Praise for *Pilgrimage as Spiritual Practice*

"Pilgrimage studies benefits from having no one academic lens controlling the conversation. There are still awkward silences when we try to address the diverse forms of spirituality that modern pilgrims long to sample. At last, we have a book by and for educators attuned to the deep longings of world travelers on sacred treks. There is consolation in the journey, a feeling of being at home in your body, in the natural world, and in your soul. This book maps freshly marked trails that bend toward transcendence."
—George Greenia, professor emeritus of modern languages, and founder, William & Mary Institute for Pilgrimage Studies

"Wayfarers of the world will delight in this new volume, which examines spiritual journeys in multiple settings and from multiple perspectives. Academics, theologians, and practitioners guide the reader and lay pilgrim on their travels of transcendence—for example, a member of the society of Jesus embarks on a Sufi pilgrimage in Senegal. Worth special mention in the handbook are the discussion guides and notes for further reading, which will be invaluable as the readers embark on their own journeys of transformation."
—Ian S. McIntosh, founder, Sacred Journeys Project

"From Senegal to Santiago, from physical training to phenomenology, this collection of essays for teachers of pilgrimage and wayfarers is as rich and varied as the landscapes and practices it explores. Bloechl and Brouillette have assembled a global list of pilgrimage scholars and wayfarers. Asceticism, art, and Ignatian spirituality share the way with practical tips on pedagogy to make this an essential collection for the teacher and pilgrimage guide."
—Matthew R. Anderson, affiliate professor, Concordia University, Montreal

"This is one of the best books on modern pilgrimage to be written in a long time. The chapters in this book highlight the pilgrim, the guide, and the teacher as the key actors in the creation of the pilgrimage experience. This volume serves as a valuable resource for those interested in both the pilgrim experience as well as the role of teachers and guides that facilitate this activity."
—Dr. Daniel H. Olsen, professor and chair, department of geography, Brigham Young University

"Indubitably, *Pilgrimage as Spiritual Practice* offers a fascinating set of essays to deepen our understanding of the theory and practice of pilgrimage. With their holistic perspective in mind, editors André Brouillette and Jeffrey Bloechl seek—and provide—answers to such ponderous questions as, 'How can teachers allow the experiences of others to inform their students' pilgrimage paths?' The annotated bibliographical sources and the questions for further reflection make this book essential reading and contribute mightily to its overall usefulness."
—E. Moore Quinn, professor of anthropology, College of Charleston

"At the heart of *Pilgrimage as Spiritual Practice* is a marvelous idea: a gathering together of scholarly, personal, and practical reflections on pilgrimage. The chapters are beautifully written, accessible accounts that range across academic disciplines and religious traditions. This volume will be a vital resource for pilgrims of all levels of experience."
—Simon Coleman, Chancellor Jackman Professor, University of Toronto

PILGRIMAGE
AS SPIRITUAL PRACTICE

PILGRIMAGE
as Spiritual Practice

A Handbook for Teachers, Wayfarers, and Guides

Editors

Jeffrey Bloechl
André Brouillette

Fortress Press
Minneapolis

Contents

PART 2: CONTEXTS

Acknowledgments

The journey toward this book started in the summer of 2015 with a pilgrimage for Boston College faculty members—each of whom would eventually lead a pilgrimage course for students. The course has benefited annually from the support of the Boston College Office of Student Formation; Gregory Kalscheur, SJ, dean of the Morrissey College of Arts and Sciences; and David Quigley, provost of the university. Years later, as we were shaping a book project with a group of pilgrim scholars, Scott Tunseth at Fortress Press welcomed it wholeheartedly and guided its initial steps. For our research and a conference, we benefited from the support of various entities at Boston College: the School of Theology and Ministry, the Department of Philosophy at the Morrissey College of Arts and Sciences, and the Office of Student Formation. Graduate student Abbey Murphy contributed to the initial editing of the texts. We are grateful to Will Bergkamp at Fortress Press and his team for the pleasant experience of working with them to bring this book to light.

Introduction

Anyone who has been on a long pilgrimage will remember the considerable enthusiasm and interest with which, upon one's return, others pose certain questions, ask for recommendations of a text or a film about the topic, and often enough, begin to draw up their own plans for a long walk. As pleasant as this is, it raises some difficulties. The pilgrim knows well that no two experiences of pilgrimage are quite the same and that, indeed, on many occasions there are few rules in place (though plenty of mores and habits). This is also the case for *thinking about* pilgrimage, whether in the mode of reflection from within the practice or from a more interpretive distance. And so those who would lead a pilgrimage or teach a course that may involve one are not evidently placed to speak about it in definitive terms. The ordinary pilgrim cautions time and again that what they have just said is only an expression of one person's perspective. The teacher and the guide must also observe that it has been necessary to favor a particular wisdom, focus on a particular context and form, and choose a particular perspective or discipline. If the teacher and guide happen to be especially adept, they might integrate more than one.

The title of this volume, *Pilgrimage as Spiritual Practice*, begs the question of spirituality. Most pilgrimages have religious roots, but pilgrims undertake them for a variety of reasons and, more often than not, with a certain spiritual overtone. Considering pilgrimage as a "spiritual practice" suggests that unlike a purely physical activity, or a purely intellectual one, the practice of pilgrimage calls forth the whole person (physically, emotionally, intellectually, religiously, etc.). Pilgrims are often invited to situate themselves anew, through the experience, in their relationship with their purpose in life, in their place in a group or relations with others (fellow pilgrims, hosts, etc.), in their rapport to creation, to landscape (in urban or wilderness settings), to memory and history, and potentially to God or to other religious figures. A certain sense of transcendence, of going beyond oneself while being wholly implicated in an actual experience, is what we understand as a spiritual practice.

We have sought to recognize the complications of the multiplicity of perspectives on pilgrimage in the collection of essays that fill this volume. Each of them includes a dimension of personal experience, as pilgrim and as teacher or guide. They weave a scholarly reflection to enhance the understanding of the experience. Some essays are focused by what we have just called context or form (the Camino de Santiago de Compostela, the Shikoku Henro, etc.). Others are instead focused by a commitment especially to the methods of one discipline (psychology, art history, etc.). These two groups plainly overlap each other at many important points. The essays also pay special attention to the pedagogical or formative dimension of pilgrimage. On the practical side, each essay offers some questions for reflection as well as an annotated bibliography to suggest further readings related to the theme. We do not pretend to have covered the field but hope to have cleared a small place from which to make one's way into more of it.

Our aim, as editors, has been to provide something of a handbook by which the ordinary pilgrim may explore different experiences and modes of reflection and by which teachers and guides may begin to identify resources and approaches for their own efforts. Individual readers can certainly deepen their understanding of the pilgrimage phenomenon through the insights of the various disciplines or the different contextual journeys. Groups can prepare an upcoming pilgrimage or explore more theoretically the theme of pilgrimage by having lively discussions with the help of the questions for reflection. Teachers or guides can also make use of the bibliographies to enhance and renew their input to their groups. Would-be pilgrims might even be inspired to take the step of making a pilgrimage.

Let us follow a single thread into the volume rather than simply cut through the order laid down in our table of contents. Our efforts were prompted by a discussion between Jeffrey Bloechl, professor of philosophy at Boston College, and Mary Jo Kietzman, professor of English literature at the University of Michigan–Flint. It is our pleasure to conclude this volume with Kietzman's moving essay on urban pilgrimage in a city so greatly shaken by recent calamity and yet so hopeful and resilient (chapter 12). The logical counterpart of her essay has been contributed by Kip Redick, professor of philosophy and religious studies at Christopher Newport University (chapter 11). Redick is among the most prominent—and, we dare suggest, most untiring—scholars and teachers of walking. His interpretation of pilgrimage in nature is borne of considerable experience and suggests important links with modern philosophy. The latter is also the point of departure for the essay that opens this volume (chapter 1) by Jeffrey Bloechl. Bloechl proposes a straightforward phenomenological account of pilgrimage. What are its necessary conditions? What is it, and what is it not? But this does not yet reach the question of personal capacity, and so we cannot do without the analyses—empirical, theoretical, developmental—undertaken by Heather Warfield, who teaches clinical and counseling psychology at Antioch University (chapter 3). A pilgrimage, she observes, can be a journey of self-discovery and growth. Teachers and guides are therefore also facilitators. Of course, positive outcomes are not guaranteed, and what one may originally think is negative may well have important lessons of its own. Pilgrimage is often a struggle, in other words, but the struggle is often the source of what is best and lasting. Moreover, this often occurs in the company of others (where is the pilgrim who has not sometimes considered fellow wayfarers a mixed blessing?). Eileen Sweeney, also a philosopher at Boston College, addresses these difficult themes, and others close to them, head-on and with a wonderful nod or two to Chaucer (chapter 5).

What sustains us along the way? For Kathryn Barush, an art historian, and Hung Pham, SJ, a specialist in Ignatian spirituality (collaborating at the Graduate Theological Union in Berkeley), this must include what we find recorded by those who have gone before—what they have found so important as to render in works of art that are at once a testimony to the riches of a tradition and an inspiration to courage and creativity in the living present (chapter 4). As for tradition, it hardly needs saying that some of the world's great pilgrimages are embedded in an entire ensemble of principles and practices that make up a distinctive way of life, even as it also enriches and transforms our understanding of them. It is no mistake that a number of contributors to this volume are members of the Society of Jesus, whose founder, Ignatius of Loyola, referred to himself as "the pilgrim" in the narrative of his life's journey. This is a leitmotif of the essay by André Brouillette, SJ, a theologian at Boston College (chapter 2), seen this time through a Russian spiritual classic. Christianity has always included a place for the pilgrimage practice, including in its Scriptures, and a study of pilgrims and pilgrimage conducts one toward the heart of Christian theology.

Christianity is hardly the only tradition in which there is a close relation between the practice of pilgrimage and what we might call, for the sake of brevity, an essential doctrine and spirituality. In his essay, "India: The Pilgrim People" (chapter 6), Yann Vagneux, MEP, a scholar-priest who has lived in Benares for many years, reminds us of an identification that in India one may venture without exaggeration. Pilgrimages well known for both daunting severity and unsurpassed beauty trace the lineaments of a worldview. To walk toward the sources of the great Ganges is at the same time to enact an inner journey toward the Absolute. So likewise, farther east, in Japan, does walking enact a way of being, and so likewise is the theme of asceticism prominent there. In "The Steepness of the Pilgrim Path" (chapter 8), John Shultz, professor of Asian religion and philosophy at Kansai Gaidai University, traces this principle both back into the history of Japanese religion, where accounts of long pilgrimages of great physical and mental challenge proliferate, and forward from there to reflections on the manner in which a guided pilgrimage—to be sure, in the extraordinary beauty of the Japanese mountains—can seize upon those challenges to draw a wayfarer into a deep sense of the spirituality that has embraced the practice for many centuries. This is at least equally the case in Islam, in which the hajj is at once a distinctive practice and a canonical feature of the entire faith. For Albertus Bagus Laksana, SJ, an Indonesian theologian, the recurrent theme is an opportunity for comparison and, in turn, enriched understanding (chapter 7). Followers of Ignatius of Loyola are neither the only nor even the first to recognize in *peregrinatio* a means to recover one's most profound relation to God, creation, and others. Indeed, an encounter with the robust orientation to relations with others that was profiled by Ghazali at the dawn of the second millennium cannot fail to return us to dimensions of the Christian experience that might otherwise remain undervalued. Another comparative exercise recorded in this volume is undertaken by Norbert Litoing, SJ, a Harvard-educated anthropologist who has led many student groups along the Sufi pilgrimage route to Xóotoum Ngor in Senegal (chapter 9). As a scholar and a practicing Catholic, Litoing's walks bring his own faith into contact with that of another tradition and at the same time place the entire matter of faith, and its worldview, in some tension with the very different worldview engendered by his scholarship.

In this volume, we have accorded ample space for teachers and guides, because we know from our own experience that the pilgrim who chooses that role is called upon to think and to speak with somewhat more explicit attention to a number of variables that the ordinary pilgrim may be content to leave unthematized. This is the explicit concern of "This Is the Way" (chapter 10), co-authored by James Barber and Benjamin Boone of the College of William and Mary, which has promoted courses involving pilgrimage along the Camino de Santiago for nearly twenty years. Drawing on an immense store of data and reflection, they address a range of important considerations, as it were, from start to finish of an academic course that includes a pilgrimage experience. Not least of these is the task of simply understanding the expectations and desires of those who one will lead. This point, we submit, is on the minds of all of the authors contributing to this volume and, indeed, was raised early by Mary Jo Kietzman in the conversations that sparked the entire project.

Jeffrey Bloechl and André Brouillette, SJ
Chestnut Hill, Massachusetts
September 2021

PART 1

Approaches

Chapter 1

A Brief Phenomenology of Pilgrimage

Jeffrey Bloechl
Boston College

Some Preliminary Notes on Walking

The first thing to understand about pilgrimage is that it is unlike the ordinary forms of walking. Since what is ordinary is most familiar to us, in order to see what pilgrimage truly is, we will have to make it appear strange. We manage some progress with this task if we take our guidance from the words that name different forms of the acting that is walking. But if we stop there, we will not get to the fact that these words also express ways of being in the world. The philosophy that is phenomenology, with its insistence on getting to "the things themselves," helps us reach a level of occurrence that is prior to the question of understanding what we hope are the right names or concepts for things.

As it happens, regarding pilgrimage, there are immediate problems with the attempt to take some guidance from the words we use. To begin with, at least in English, there is no evident verb. We say that one wanders, tours, perambulates, and so forth, but we do not say that one "pilgrims" or perhaps "pilgrimates," and it will not help much to appeal to the Latin *peregrinus*, from which we have both "pilgrim" and "peregrination." For the most part, "peregrination" has the sense of roaming or traipsing about (though in a more arcane English, the word does have a religious resonance). The bare fact that pilgrimage appears to be something other than this takes us to one of its primary conditions: pilgrimage is movement in a singular and determined way. Moreover, in this much, it touches on what some would have us recognize as a primary metaphor in human consciousness.[1] A great deal of our being and doing would be unintelligible without it. Consider the simple practice of crossing a crowded room, a town, or an open field but also the undertaking of a complex task and even the effort to think through a problem: all of these seem to require, and spontaneously invoke, a sense of moving deliberately forward along a line in a specific direction. Perhaps this helps us understand the unusual power that pilgrimage exercises on our imagination. To go on pilgrimage is to enter into a particular practice and even a formation that readies one for it, in which our full selves belong to something as fundamental as moving along a determined way. One feels immediately that there is much more to be said about this, but for the moment it is enough to note only a profound resonance between pilgrimage—probably along with certain other forms of wayfaring—and the primitive conditions of our being.

Let us take one step back from these few thoughts to consider the suggestion that movement is not merely the crossing of space in the flow of time—or rather, that it is not originally that. The Greek philosophers knew this. Their word *kinesis* conceives of a

---

1. For the phenomenological development of the "way" as a primary metaphor, see Erazim Kohak, "Of Dwelling and Wayfaring," in *The Longing for Home*, ed. Leroy S. Rouner (South Bend, IN: University of Notre Dame Press, 1997), 30–46. (I thank Stephen Ferguson for this reference.) For a similar conception of the related theme of the "road," see Jim Forest, *Road the Emmaus: Pilgrimage as a Way of Life* (Maryknoll, NY: Orbis, 2007), 3.

basic change from potentiality to actuality, of which the change that is of place is only one form. They also frame the word in an experience of nature as seeking its own fulfillment. Natural change is the movement of growth and flourishing. Obviously, there can be corrupt or deficient change, but this is a departure from one's nature.

When phenomenology takes up these themes in Greek thought, it is with a view strictly to interpreting the movement of human beings in a world, among things, and with one another.[2] Moreover, with few exceptions, phenomenology leaves aside any attempt to understand this movement in relation to human fulfillment or a highest good. For Heidegger, in fact, the movement of one's being must be understood in relation to its end in one's own death. We are not bound to accept this restriction, but one may find in it a useful starting point from which to card out pilgrimage from similar instances of what I have just called "wayfaring." In order to do this, I appeal to a distinction between what is *initial* in our being and acting and what may prove to take exception from the initial. If, as phenomenology enjoins, we begin from the initial—from what is most familiar and, in that sense, ordinary—we are led first to recognize that pilgrimage is, in some sense, to be sure, a practice of our movement in the world. This helps us see what many accounts of pilgrimage identify as essential: it is precisely *not* limited to our relation with the world or, in starker terms, *not* limited to the relation with our own death, through which the world is interpreted only with a view to going on living.

---

2. This occurs especially in the phenomenology of Heidegger. He appropriates Aristotle in this way already in a 1922 study of Aristotle meant to outline a research program that anticipates important features of *Being and Time*. Change, being-moved (*kinesis*), is understood to proceed from lack (*steresis*), which is interpreted, with regard to Dasein, as the having of one's own death. See Martin Heidegger, "Phenomenological Interpretations with Respect to Aristotle: Indications of the Hermeneutic Situation," trans. Michael Baur, in *Man and World* 25, nos. 3–4 (1992): 390.

Needless to say, there are other practices that break free of governance by the care and concern of mortal existence. There is the carefree meandering of the sightseer, the detached wandering of the urban *flâneur*, and the more elevated, conversational strolling sometimes enjoined by Cicero in his *Tusculan Disputations*.[3] A comparative phenomenology of walking might begin with examples like these and seek the place of pilgrimage among them.[4] A course on pilgrimage might have students enter into this same exercise experientially (a walk in the city, a walk together in a park, etc.). One quickly realizes that most of these practices suspend ordinary conditions only so far as to make it possible for us to stand back from the entanglement in the world that they project. The sightseer wishes to see the ordinary world a little differently, or more vividly, but not at all in order to contest its limits. When Baudelaire or Pessoa wander the city streets at night, it is from an alienated restlessness but not evidently from a longing for anything more than private consolation. And when Cicero paced the parks of Rome with a student or peer, the goal was simply to turn aside distractions that prevent good minds from spurring one another to deeper insight and improved discourse.

---

3. On the *flâneur*, see Charles Baudelaire, "Tableaux parisiens," available in English in *Selected Poems*, trans. Carol Clark (Harmondsworth, UK: Penguin, 1995). The figure also is present, though much more fleetingly, in Fernando Pessoa, *Book of Disquiet*, trans. Richard Zenith (Harmondsworth, UK: Penguin, 2002), 14, 45, 68–70, and so on. Cicero seems to have distinguished the learning that requires sitting from the sort that is best undertaken while walking together. The practice was urban and civic, undertaken in gardens with a colonnade. An example of the latter is found in the first of the *Tusculan Disputations*.

4. To my knowledge, we do not yet have quite such a thing. However, one will find useful indications in the well-known little book by Frédéric Gros, *A Philosophy of Walking* (London: Verso, 2017), and a much larger, more personal one by Bruce Baugh entitled *Philosophers' Walks* (New York: Routledge, 2021).

This same comparative effort would also have to give some attention to tourism, in which one does cross out and cross over the boundaries—some conventional, some natural—that mark ordinary space. Yet this is motivated only to get *somewhere else*, whether this has either the negative form of escaping from home or else the more positive form of seeking a better understanding of nature or culture. The travel of the tourist is not always sheer exoticism but more generally a form of circulation within knowable limits. It is also, as the travel writer Paul Theroux has often observed, a mindset more than an activity. One goes from "here" to "there," and at the moment one arrives "there," the "there" has already become another "here"—or at least another facet or dimension of the expanding here that is made up of what is familiar. In no case does the tourist truly call into question the authority of this simple distinction between here and there over our relation to the world as such. As I will suggest, there is good reason to think that pilgrimage does precisely this.

All of that said, in our attempts to distinguish pilgrimage from these different practices of walking, we should not lose sight of the fact that nearly any true pilgrim does spend parts of each day, for better or worse, on sightseeing; wandering aimlessly in villages and towns, lost in deep conversation with others; and unabashedly touring Galicia, Tuscany, and other fascinating and beautiful places. This is simply a matter of fact, but recognizing it helps us avoid reducing the composite experience of the pilgrim only to an ideal definition. The practice is rich and complex. Its first order of business is not simply visiting new places or talking with new people, and its ongoing nature is not immediately lost when, as is inevitable, one is captivated by a stunning landscape or deeply moved by the sharing of hearts that sometimes happens among companions on the way. Moreover, as many pilgrims report, it may eventually happen that we cease to think of these experiences as interruptions or distractions and instead find them to be fully consistent with the central practice. To be sure, one still wanders off, physically or mentally, but one begins to feel that what happens then—and whom one encounters—truly belongs to a landscape that one inhabits prior to any geography.

It is not especially difficult to see what makes this difference. The pilgrim, as pilgrim, is found on the way toward some good that is sufficiently desirable as to have motivated setting aside the pursuit of those goods that are sought in other forms of walking. Let us briefly revisit the Greek notion of a movement that is fundamental to our being, and let us admit the idea that its initial condition is to circulate within the limits of what is accessible within the world. This can be said in plain language: we move first, spontaneously, toward finite things that please and satisfy us. The nature of this movement is not seriously altered by the other forms of walking that we have touched on. To meander from one site to another, and even to do so while immersed in good conversation, is, quite arguably, to repeat on another level, or with new sophistication, our most ordinary movement. If, in contrast, the pilgrim moves toward some good that transcends those goods that please us and satisfy us, then as a practice, it promotes a form of movement that somehow alters the movement that I have called the initial—which, after all, comes spontaneously. Of course, to anyone who has undertaken a lengthy pilgrimage, this is perfectly evident. One puts up with a great deal, physically and mentally, for something that not only is elusive for a long time but may even prove to be something else entirely than what one had originally expected. Those who are puzzled or repelled by pilgrimage probably do not grasp this important feature. If it is not raised early with students and aspirants—if one does not in some way raise the question of a highest good or value,[5] if one does not ask early and often, "What finally do you want from this, after all, fairly arduous experience?"—there is a considerable chance that they will soon become confused, lethargic, and even resistant to daily immersion in the elements, spare and simple food, and an entire array of aches and pains. Conversely, if one does raise it, and if it is truly heard, there is instead some chance that an entire scale of lesser goods will unfold in light of the greater one that lies always ahead of those lesser goods that are given along the way toward the highest one (whatever it turns out to be). Some of these lesser goods nurture us in important ways and are cause for easy gratitude: hot tea, a quiet smile from a passing stranger, gentle rain after an especially blistering afternoon. Others test us and are cause for patience: food that is not fully to one's liking, an overly crowded path, intense heat until late in the day. Of course, sometimes bad food just is bad food and crowds along a narrow path just are inconvenient. But for the pilgrim who has embraced a guiding intention for the walk, these reactions also say something about a natural and ongoing struggle to fully commit to it. This sometimes makes the reactions themselves useful portals for personal discernment.

A long discussion could be had over whether this shift of orientation elevates the initial movement of our being by directing it to something better or only transforms it without necessarily improving it. We still can make progress, phenomenologically

---

5. The choice of terms is fraught with complication. Those of a certain faith are inclined to speak frankly of a path to God. Those of a more metaphysical mindset may think more readily of a desire for the highest good, and those of a more psychological bent may prefer the language of value. I have found that during the early stages of a group pilgrimage, it is best to leave these differences intact so that reflection and conversation may continue without excluding anyone.

(and, I think, pedagogically), if we only take note of the change. It has seemed that a number of practices that appear to resemble pilgrimage (strolling, wandering, exploring) are carried out within the world of goods that we may reach by our own powers. They do not contest, let alone breach the limit of, what I have been calling "the ordinary"—that is, the limit of acts, events, or things that can be considered alongside one another, as if side by side within a single horizon.[6] Pilgrimage, in contrast, opens itself to something "extraordinary," which is to say something beyond all other things, in the sense of being desirable in a way that encourages one to raise it above one's investment in all of those other things. As we have seen, those other things are not given up entirely but recast in light of something that transcends them. Another long discussion could be had over quite how to understand and name what thus transcends, but one thing is clear: it is our relation with it, and not with the world we start from, that has the ultimate word on what a pilgrimage will mean. When on pilgrimage, the world and everything in it make up what is specifically *penultimate*.[7]

The Hermeneutics of Penultimacy

It may be useful to repeat that there are philosophical and pedagogical reasons for suspending the question of what truly defines the highest good or value, which on group pilgrimages is certain to raise complex theological and spiritual debate. If by "philosophy" we mean "phenomenology," then we begin from and stay as close as

---

6. I am appealing to simple etymology. *Ordinary:* usual, customary, in conformity with a regulated sequence or arrangement. See *Oxford Dictionary of English* (Oxford: Oxford University Press, 1966).

7. The expression is the subject of the fifth chapter of Dietrich Bonhoeffer's *Ethics*, trans. N. H. Smith (New York: Touchstone, 1985), 120–85; the German term is *das Vorletzte*. I have come to understand its philosophical significance from the important work of Jean-Yves Lacoste.

possible to the manner in which the life that informs the practice appears to us. For as long as possible, we ask only about what can be seen and refrain from making claims about dimensions that cannot be seen—which is not at all to say that they are not real and do not have an intelligibility of their own. This still leaves a great deal of work to do.

We have been able to see this much: pilgrimage does not concede to the order and demands of the world but also does not pretend to fully escape them. To be on pilgrimage is still to be in a world and even, existentially, to have a world, but now in the mode of not belonging entirely to it. What does this look like in flesh and bone? It is not only that one's world is no longer organized as if to make a home in it, but instead, it takes shape as a space opened toward some point of distant arrival. Things and even nourishments undergo a similar transformation. It is true that a good pair of shoes and a stick of the right length to support my poor back and legs are simply tools defined by the use I make of them, yet on pilgrimage, the existential care that they serve is itself submitted to a relation with something that one feels must lie beyond immediate conditions—and this we see most vividly in the moving images of pilgrims who carry on through great frailty and indeed sometimes start in that condition. As for food, there is more than folk wisdom in the basic precautions we take on a long pilgrimage: avoid rich food, sugar, and alcohol in favor of simple fruits and vegetables; consume perhaps more carbohydrates than usual; and drink a great deal of water. To some degree, then, eating and drinking are stripped down closer to the basic nutrition that will enable one simply to go on living, and that in turn is in the service of moving toward some transcendent good. As distinct from the idea that the world and things are defined in terms only of our initial condition, in pilgrimage we witness a turn from implementality to something more like provisionality. Or rather, the sense in which a thing is implemental is subordinated to a sense in which it is provisional.

There are other changes to consider. The experience of one's own body, in its immediacy and its schematization according to a distinct set of practices, deserves close attention. This is especially interesting when considered in relation to its intersubjective dimension. Blisters, sunburn, muscle aches, and worse are physical reminders of a more profound woundedness that some religious traditions consider to be our authentic condition. One might certainly glorify them, in which case they will probably feed into an egotism that opposes itself to any real sense of community. But our various wounds may also work against pride and insularity so that the moment when one must ask for help becomes an occasion of greater intimacy with those who might offer it. It is difficult to imagine that this does not befall any group pilgrimage, and when it does, it often has a powerful effect on those few who start out in full confidence of their strength and toughness only to have these eventually fail. One by one, the members of a group learn that they are only as efficient and as fast moving as the slowest among them and that literally any one among them might find himself or herself in that latter condition for a time. In theological-political terms, a group of pilgrims truly committed to walking together is no mere plurality of individuals. Considered in their corporeality, they appear much more like what Paul of Tarsus calls the body of Christ (1 Cor 12:12–27; Rom 12:5–6). Moreover, as Paul himself notes, the weakest among us may prove to be the most important. After all, in them the truth is clearest.

Of course, what was admitted earlier about different forms of movement must also be admitted about different relations to the world, things, one's own body, and other people: each pilgrim shifts frequently among these different modalities in any given hour, day, or week. However, this does not mean that a pilgrim is simply adrift among them. At least some of the time, it is instead a matter of concentrated effort—or again, practice—and the contrary effects of fatigue, indolence, and distraction. There is good reason to forgive oneself for struggling with this, since after all, what it comes down to is an effort to curb and eventually disempower an attitude and habits that do serve us well in ordinary life. For those who walk long enough, there is no getting away from some form of surrender, since sooner or later, it becomes difficult to summon practical reasons to continue (though I will confess long moments in which I have been sustained only by the desperately practical thought that carrying on is the easiest and least embarrassing way to bring it to an end).

The last thing to surrender is a comfortable certainty that one already knows what it will all have meant and how it must end. This stands to reason as soon as pilgrimage appears in terms of struggle and surrender, each of which can be traced to the question of what to do with one's own ego. Here the difficulty no longer lies with the robust egotism that glories in its own suffering and achievement but instead lies in the subtle insistence of a wish to master the situation by comprehending it in advance. It is when the surrender of this wish is necessarily linked to a desire for some highest good that pilgrimage looks most emphatically like spiritual practice. Perhaps it is possible to work on this surrender directly, by one or another mental strategy for rejecting idols. To my knowledge, this is attempted much more frequently among contemplatives and monastic ascetics, where a doctrine and community provide stability and respite. Even there, the path is sometimes understood as pilgrimage, as when the followers of Bruno of Cologne—the Carthusians—call themselves "pilgrims of the absolute." Somewhat in this same line, more identifiable lessons can be taken from Francis of Assisi and

Ignatius of Loyola, each of whom discovered his lasting vocation only after having had to realize that what he truly wanted was not what he had assumed it to be and each of whom consequently identified himself as a "pilgrim."[8] Francis found God in all things only after he surrendered his cherished notion of a fierce and demanding God for whom one should be willing to die at any moment. For Ignatius, who resembles Francis more than one sometimes hears, a similar decisive insight came upon the failure of a literal pilgrimage to Jerusalem with his companions. For both, pilgrimage becomes a figure of life itself, without any end that would be in our reach.

It has sometimes seemed to me that we more modest pilgrims approach this final surrender when we enter into the monotony that characterizes the regular schedule and concerns that are required to walk great distances day upon day. It is probably inevitable that the pilgrim will fall prey to the boredom that accompanies it, as if it were already lying in wait somewhere along the *meseta* between Burgos and Leon on the Camino de Santiago or certain vast and arid fields in the Tuscan portion of the Via Francigena. There must certainly be a heavy, labored side to this, but one can sometimes detect a side that appears to be something else entirely. One catches sight of the former, labored side of monotony as the persistence of physical and mental challenges weakens and, in some cases, entirely destroys one's early enthusiasm for the walk. Enchantment with nature, culture, and companions likewise declines. The path itself no longer feels like a way into new discoveries so much as a line simply to be followed. It is true, of course, that one has freely chosen all of this, but it is also true that that freedom looks increasingly like submission to a singular task. Surprisingly, this very situation

---

8. From the moment of his conversion, Francis dressed in a simple robe, carried a long stick, and lived an itinerant life. Ignatius calls himself "the pilgrim" throughout his autobiography.

Camino de Santiago de Compostela, Portomarín.
Photo by Holly Vandewall.

can also yield such a pleasure that some pilgrims I have known describe the monotony itself as what they miss most upon returning to ordinary life. Now, unless this pleasure is only relief at having briefly escaped a dissipated and hectic life (and in many cases, this is surely at least one part of it), we must consider the unexpected possibility that there is something positive in the monotony itself. Let us start with the fact that it is precisely not a mode of engagement with anything that has previously gratified this or that ordinary desire. But let us also refrain from the claim, dubious in the extreme, that it would already be an arrival at the good for which we have been willing to suspend the gratification of all such desires. This is enough for us to see that monotony is intermediate or transitional, between the "no longer" of a previous mode and the "not yet" of what one still seeks. Of course, it is also undecided, without a necessary trajectory: we very often quickly recoil from monotony back into some form of the previous, worldly mode of engagement, but on other occasions, we remain there for some considerable time, and in the rarest of these we may even pass over into a deep serenity with what simply must be the case. There is no single cause for these different outcomes. When I have been plagued by back problems, it has been all but impossible not to withdraw especially from monotony, let alone fervor, into dreams of a chance to give it all up for a good bed and meal anywhere else than in the prescribed locations. Yet when my body has felt strong and resilient, I have been able to commit it to the schedule and the trail without further need of attention and thus let my thoughts flow freely. As for my mind, when the dull pattern of each day leaves me alone with preoccupations that are too powerful or complex to gather into focus, I am inclined to strike up idle chatter or indulge in extended daydreaming. When my mind has settled, I am able to find my way through any kind of boredom into genuine conversation and deep reflection.

If we recognize that this ease of body and mind comes only when one's full self is entirely, without distraction or reservation, committed to the way, and if we understand that in order to reach such a condition we must first fully disentangle ourselves from everything that might cause distraction or reservation, then we have identified the importance of monotony. In monotony, one has come loose from the everyday world and thus open to another possibility of being there.

It is worth emphasizing that the rare pilgrim who proceeds from ordinary engagement through monotony to serenity has along the way given up a claim to possess a full understanding of its meaning and outcome. This does not mean that one knows nothing or that one no longer has any reason or motive for carrying on. But to the degree that pilgrimage opposes itself to egocentricity, it does mean that one does not actually possess the reason or control the motive. These are given to us from beyond ourselves, either in the strong sense that rests on a doctrine and a teaching about a transcendent source or only in the weaker sense of what just *is*. Whichever the case, the walking is essentially a response to them. And in the end, the practice aims to be *only* and *purely* a response. The pilgrim who reaches this far would go fully into that practice, all the way until perfect conformity with its conditions. This brings us close to what Thoreau may have in mind when, in his lecture called "Walking," he envisions a movement that takes aim at beatitude precisely by refusing anything other than the activity itself.[9] If I have understood him well, and if what he suggests is truly possible, then at least one important end of pilgrimage has little to do with the completion of

9. This way of reading Thoreau is controversial and makes much of his interest in Indian thought. I have found it worked out in Alan Hodder, *Thoreau's Ecstatic Witness* (New Haven, CT: Yale University Press, 2001).

a journey drawn on our maps. It may even be the case that at some point, maps are simply in the way.

Bear Lake, Wisconsin
March 2021

Questions for Reflection

1. What distinguishes different forms of walking? What might characterize each of them as a habit or practice?
2. What features of ordinary life must be carried on in the extraordinary activity of pilgrimage? How might their meaning be altered there?
3. What do I want most or value most in life? To what am I ultimately called? What supports me in answering this call, and what hinders me?
4. How is this sketch of my life (question 3) repeated in pilgrimage? What do I want most from pilgrimage? What calls me to pilgrimage? What might help and hinder me along the way?

Select Annotated Bibliography

Bonhoeffer, Dietrich. *Ethics*. Translated by N. H. Smith. New York: Touchstone, 1985.
> Chapter 5 is an extended theological reflection on the relation between penultimate and ultimate things.
Evagrius Ponticus. *The Praktikos* (in many editions).
> Evagrius's account of *acedia* is an excellent point of departure for reflection on profound monotony and boredom. A concise definition is given at § 12.

Forest, Jim. *Road the Emmaus: Pilgrimage as a Way of Life*. Maryknoll, NY: Orbis, 2007.

Forest stays close to the central metaphors active in pilgrimage and links them to other senses of being on the way toward the supreme good in one's life. Pilgrimage is rendered an excellent point of access to a range of other religious phenomena.

Gros, Frédéric. *A Philosophy of Walking*. London: Verso, 2017.

Gros offers a clear and easily readable account of how important philosophers have found walking important, how they thought about this, and how it influenced their thinking in general.

Heidegger, Martin. *Being and Time*. Translated by Edward Robinson and John Macquarrie. London: Blackwell, 1962.

See especially §§ 14–28 for a rigorous account of the form of being in the world that pilgrimage appears to *modify* or *break from*.

Kohak, Erazim. "Of Dwelling and Wayfaring." In *The Longing for Home*, edited by Leroy S. Rouner, 30–46. South Bend, IN: University of Notre Dame Press, 1997.

Kohak's essay is an accessible means to thinking about the direction and movement of pilgrim walking both in relation to and as distinct from other forms of walking and for a claim that it appeals to a primary symbol or metaphor in human consciousness.

Marcel, Gabriel. *Homo Viator*. Translated by E. Craufurd. South Bend, IN: St. Augustine's Press, 2010.

Marcel is the North Atlantic philosopher who has argued most often that being human is necessarily being on a way. This is brought out best, though, without extended systematic development in the essays on hope, value, and immortality.

Thoreau, Henry David. "Walking" (in many anthologies).

Thoreau approaches walking as a spiritual practice intent on undoing every structure and prejudice of the everyday, customary, and conventional, thereby approaching perfect consistency with the whole that Thoreau calls "nature," "the west," and "the wild."

Chapter 2

Journey and Body

Theological Reflection from Pilgrimage

André Brouillette, SJ
Boston College

In its early years, the movement of the followers of Jesus Christ was sometimes called *hê hodos*, meaning the "way" or the "road" (e.g., Acts 9:2). Not a religion (all disciples were Jews), not a philosophy (the language of *logos* would come later), but a way of being, believing, journeying. A way to undertake and follow. Consequently, the adoption of pilgrimage praxis by the Christian tradition reveals a deep connection with the *style* of Christianity.

While pilgrimage has deep resonances with the Christian ethos and has a long history in Christianity, it never became a religious obligation. Pilgrimages nevertheless have been part of the fabric of Christianity in a great variety of shapes and forms to the present day. From visits to the apostles' tombs, through local and international walking pilgrimages in the Middle Ages, to the contemporary pilgrimages in an era of mass transportation, pilgrimages have morphed over the centuries. The landscape of Christianity, with its shrines and monasteries, was greatly shaped by the flux of pilgrims. In the realm of spirituality, pilgrimage was also elevated to the level of a metaphor for Christian life.

From an ecumenical perspective, pilgrimage is loaded with denominational differences. While Catholics and Orthodox are comfortable with this practice, Protestants and evangelicals have more misgivings about it, initially because of its rejection by the sixteenth-century Reformers. The importance of the Bible and of the place of Jerusalem nonetheless led to a newfound interest since the nineteenth century in traveling to the Holy Land, the land of Jesus. The weight of the denominational perspectives should not be discounted. My experience of pilgrimage is rooted in being a Roman Catholic and Jesuit priest from Quebec. I have done pilgrimages short (a few hours) and long (two weeks) in various cities and countries. I made some by myself, some in small groups, and others with hundreds of thousands of pilgrims. I walked, drove, or used public transit for the journey.

Pilgrimage is not intrinsically a religious activity. However, its continual embrace by Christianity reveals a powerful anthropological connection worthy of theological reflection. In this essay, I bring pilgrimage into dialogue by little touches with essential theological elements, along the lines of journey and time, body and space, and in conversation with the spiritual classic *The Way of a Pilgrim*.

Journey and Time

Pilgrimage is a journey inscribed in time. We will explore this essential dimension of the pilgrimage experience through four vantage points. First, the journey depicted in the spiritual classic *The Way of a Pilgrim*. Second, the biblical roots of pilgrimage as teleological. Third, in line with individual growth. And finally, through the lens of memory, past and present.

The Way of a Pilgrim

The Way of a Pilgrim—or *The Pilgrim's Tale*—depicts the journey of an unknown nineteenth-century Russian Orthodox pilgrim.[1] The book is now considered a classic of Orthodox spirituality and an entryway into the teachings of the *Philokalia*, a collected work from the eighteenth century that features authors spanning from the church fathers to medieval theologians and saints. The pilgrimage component of the book is clearly central, not acting simply as a metaphor for another journey, unlike John Bunyan's *Pilgrim's Progress*. Another spiritual classic, the *Testament* (a.k.a. the *Autobiography*) of Ignatius of Loyola, narrates the central part of his life as a multilayered pilgrimage, though an actual pilgrimage to Jerusalem figures prominently.[2] Like for Bunyan and Ignatius, the journey of *The Way of a Pilgrim* is an interior one.

The journey of this Russian pilgrim was initiated by a desire to learn to pray without ceasing, following the Pauline injunction (1 Thess 5:17). Hence his quest was a deeply spiritual and personal one. The journey led him to hear the teachings of various clergymen on prayer. He moved on from one to another, as he was unsatisfied. The physical movement accompanied the spiritual quest. The encounter and guidance of a wise starets on the road to a monastery and a months-long stay in a quiet place offered the pilgrim the key to reach unceasing prayer with the Jesus prayer.

His pilgrimage was also guided by a corresponding desire to reach holy places: Irkutsk, Kyiv, and finally Jerusalem as a horizon.

---

1. For the context and the discussion about the authorship, see the introduction to Aleksei Pentkovsky, ed., *The Pilgrim's Tale* (New York: Paulist Press, 1999); hereafter cited as PT.
2. Ignatius of Loyola, *A Pilgrim's Testament: The Memoirs of Saint Ignatius of Loyola*, ed. Barton T. Geger, SJ (Boston: Institute of Jesuit Sources, 2020).

The destination is a magnet, and allusions to a journey to Jerusalem are important, but they do not form the main draw of the narrative.

The pilgrim started from a place of grief: loss of family, wealth, and eventually his wife. Deprived of all that was humanly dear to him, he freed himself of everything to undertake his journey. Pilgrimage became for him a way of life, since he had no place to call home—there is no return for him. Along the way, the pilgrim met mentors and companions who guided him, shared parts of their own journeys, walked with him for a time, or were instructed by him. He was frequently edified by those who had undertaken the inner journey of prayer, even in very settled places (e.g., monk, landowner, priest, army officer). He shared with them and continued to deepen his own quest. Despite the importance of these encounters, the pilgrim frequently desired solitude and moved away from company either by retiring into a quiet place or by moving forward.

Biblical Inspiration

The sense of journey is deeply rooted in the religious ethos of Christianity and in its Judaic roots. Abraham, the father of believers, was sent on a long journey toward the Promised Land (Gen 12). He is rightly revered as the father of migrants as well. Abraham was a foreigner, a man on the move, an exile, but trusting in words of hope, in the promise of a final place for his journey. Therefore, the root experience of this journey launched by a promise is strongly teleological; it aims toward a place.

The central religious experience of the Hebrew people happened in the context of a collective movement akin to pilgrimage: the Exodus. After suffering under Egyptian bondage, the Lord led the people to a journey of liberation that entailed leaving their current home to undertake what would become a forty-year journey through the desert, under the leadership of Moses, in the direction of the Promised Land. Time is necessary for such a journey. The people transitioned from oppression to freedom. They were also constituted as a people through the covenant binding them with God and also with one another. This foundational moment has been tapped into by liberation theologies that highlight the social implications of a salvation that unfolds also—though imperfectly—in our times already as kingdom.

The experience of liberation and journey in the desert toward the Promised Land is ritually remembered in the Jewish feast of Passover. A special pilgrim meal is prescribed to be eaten with the loins girded as if ready to depart. The pilgrimage of old is then not simply an event of the past but also a reality having bearing on the present. The contemporary Jewish meal of Passover concludes with the wish to meet the following year in Jerusalem as the conclusion of a pilgrimage of restoration.

In the New Testament, the journey of the disciples of Jesus has pilgrim accents. The initial sending of the Seventy-two or the Twelve was done in a pilgrim fashion: walking two by two, with only one's clothes and sandals and without money, relying on the generosity of welcoming hosts along the way (e.g., Luke 10). The disciples came back from that experience rejoicing. With the ascension and Pentecost, a final sending of the apostles by Christ in the power of the Holy Spirit is made that has set the missionary standard of Christianity. An early apostolic encounter, that of Philip with the Ethiopian official, was also realized in the context of the return from a pilgrimage (Acts 8:26–39). Paul, a later apostle, became a standard-bearer of apostolic commitment through his many journeys by land and sea.

For there is at once an ecstatic and eschatological tension in Christianity. Believers are inscribed in an "already" but also oriented toward a "not yet." The kingdom of God is at hand, but its fulfillment is still ahead. The church, as a community of believers, is present and active on earth—as the "pilgrim Church"[3]—but it journeys toward heaven, where it will encounter fullness. This eschatological tension was already at work in the writings of Saint Augustine, who used the Latin *peregrinus* (for "foreigner," "refugee") to describe the Christian condition in *The City of God*. The life of Christ himself, called the "way" (*hodos*) by the evangelist John (John 14:6), is oriented toward the "hour" (*hôra*), the central moment of his revelation that constitutes the key to his whole life. He marched resolutely toward that moment. Christianity is not cyclical but teleological and eschatological[4] while building upon a typology of prior journeys.

Individual Growth

In its use as metaphor, pilgrimage pertains to the course of life and often spiritual growth—certainly in Bunyan, Ignatius, and *The Way of a Pilgrim*. In the Roman Catholic funeral rite, there are allusions to the end of the pilgrimage of the deceased. Similarly, the Eucharistic Prayer for Various Needs mentions the hope of Christians, as their earthly pilgrimage would come to an end, to be welcomed into an eternal dwelling to live with the Lord forever.

In practice, long pilgrimages often coincide with moments of transition. On the Camino de Santiago, many pilgrims embark on their journey after experiencing or planning major life changes: the loss of a job, grief, divorce, a setback, retirement, an important

---

3. Second Vatican Council, *"Lumen Gentium," the Dogmatic Constitution on the Church*, Vatican, November 21, 1964, https://www.vatican.va/archive/hist_councils/ii_vatican _council/documents/vat-ii_const_19641121_lumen-gentium_en.html.
4. The eschatological dimension is expressed, for example, in the celebration during the Advent season and Christmas of both the first coming of Christ and the hope for his final coming at the end of time.

anniversary, or entrance into adulthood. The pilgrimage offered literally a liminal space of separation to transition into a new phase in life.

French students from Paris walk to the Cathedral of Notre-Dame de Chartres on Palm Sunday, one week before the great spring celebration of Easter, in the footsteps of poet Charles Péguy. This long tradition federates Catholic students who could be isolated in their respective institutions, offering them a time of fraternity and sharing. The pilgrimage also marks a renewed public commitment to their faith as young adults. Similarly, and more recently, the World Youth Day pilgrimage launched by Pope John Paul II constitutes a rite of passage for an internationalized youth.[5] This pilgrimage focuses not on walking but on the encounters, the festival dimension of pilgrimage—in line with the Spanish *romería*, whose definition as "pilgrimage" includes the festive celebration at the place associated with a saint. These pilgrimages at once complement and reinforce the sacramental economy, since the sacraments present a certain journey of milestones (baptism, first communion, confirmation, marriage, or ordination). The reinforcement happens in terms of both a heightened awareness of grace (e.g., through the Eucharist and the sacrament of reconciliation) and also the consciousness of living a journey that stretches beyond oneself.

Memory

Since the journey extends over time, memory is an essential part of pilgrimage, through both the collective and individual act of remembering and the reconfiguration of memory. The pilgrimage

---

5. For many European youth, the Camino plays a similar role. As a point of encounter for youth, the ecumenical community of Taizé, in France, has been a precursor since the second half of the twentieth century. See Danièle Hervieu-Léger, *Le pèlerin et le converti: La religion en mouvement* (Paris: Flammarion, 1999).

site, the shrine, and potentially the road leading to it are pregnant with memories of past pilgrims in addition to their original memorial quality—of a saint or a holy event.[6] Pilgrimage is always a return, an inscription of oneself in a narrative started long before in one's faith community, nation, family, or personal past. The exact historicity of the accounts—they often contain some legendary elements—is less important than the fact that they are cherished by a community of memory. The destination, traditionally a shrine, anchors the journey both spatially and memorially. Jerusalem outranked in importance the other pilgrimages because of its association with Christ himself and its ancient character. Because the memory of Jesus's life is very alive, places associated with him have a particular relevance.

The memorial dimension does not pertain only to the shrine or the journey of past pilgrims; it is expressed in the retelling of one's journey in pilgrimage. *The Way of a Pilgrim* is set as a series of tales or letters written by the pilgrim to his spiritual director. Through the narration of the pilgrimage, it is the self that is narrated and constructed. Nowadays, memoirs about personal pilgrimages abound. Most are not simply travel narratives but attempts at understanding oneself through the medium of telling/retelling in a narrative. The journey is then the medium and foil for the narrative (re)construction of the self. An early example of such a retelling is the *Testament* of Ignatius of Loyola, in which being a pilgrim—initially to Jerusalem—becomes in the narrative the key to understanding Ignatius's whole life.

---

6. On the shrine, see Pontifical Council for the Pastoral Care of Migrants and Itinerant People, "The Shrine: Memory, Presence and Prophecy of the Living God," Vatican, May 8, 1999, https://www.vatican.va/roman_curia/pontifical_councils/migrants/documents/rc_pc_migrants_doc_19990525_shrine_en.html.

In sum, as a journey in time, the pilgrimage is rooted in a desire (to go somewhere, to do something) and oriented to a telos. It espouses a process of understanding of the self grounded in memory and geared at growth. It is also traversed by a healthy tension between one's individual journey and the covenantal presence of others.

Body and Space

Pilgrimage is an embodied reality both through one's body and through the space moved into. We will explore this theme first through the central Christian tenet of the incarnation, then through the body narrative of the Russian pilgrim. Pilgrimage as embodied also plays out in places to go and the relics they usually hold, whose holiness calls for a response from the pilgrim. Finally, we will explore the connection between the sacrament of the Eucharist as a sacred meal born in a pilgrimage experience.

Incarnation

The *Logos* "became flesh and dwelt among us" (John 1:14). This is one of the greatest claims of the Christian message. In Jesus Christ, God became incarnate by the Holy Spirit and was a genuine human being in all dimensions—except sin. This bold claim, in the face of the divine ineffability maintained in the Jewish tradition, has tremendous consequences for the dignity of human beings and the natural world. The unfathomable distance with the divine was abolished and God made close at hand.

The incarnation highlights the dignity of the body. Hebrew Scriptures had already considered it divinely created, brought to life by God's breath (Gen 2:7). The dichotomy between body and soul that pervades Christianity was inherited from Greek philosophical influences, which tended to value the soul above the body, spirit over matter. In Christianity, the "real" person is also body, for even God, in Christ, had a body. The Apostles' Creed, stating the core tenets of the Christian faith, proclaims the belief in the "resurrection of the body"—and even, more literally, of the "flesh" (*sarx*). The body, not only the soul, is to be risen, for the human person is a temple of the Holy Spirit (1 Cor 6:19), inhabited by God's Spirit, and as such is worthy of divine inhabitation.

For Christ, the body is not simply an extraneous garment; it is the *locus* of enduring encounters. The risen body of Christ bore the marks of the cross (John 20:26–27). The scars of his life are not erased from the body. It is in the flesh that the divine life was lived out, with emotions, eating and drinking, speaking, hearing, touching, and healing. The divine experience is not lived away from the body. It is embodied, marked by the vulnerability of encounters.

Contemporary pilgrims, especially walking pilgrims, strongly experience their bodies. Pilgrimage is not first and foremost an intellectual endeavor. One experiences the limitations of the body: its strength and endurance but also its fatigue, injuries, illness, hunger, or thirst. The body can be broken, and one does not escape from it. The surroundings affect the body: the blazing sun, the drizzling rain, the cool morning, the gentle breeze. Pilgrims journey in creation, at the confluence of it. It carries uncertainties and risks.

The body opens the possibility of encounters with fellow pilgrims, hosts, or bystanders. Through ephemeral contacts or longstanding relationships, a wide and diffuse community can be established, a communal body of fellow travelers and enablers. A body with its fragility, its disappointments, its brokenness, but also its common purpose.

The Body of the Russian Pilgrim

For the pilgrim of *The Pilgrim's Tale*, the body played an essential role. As a pilgrim, he was in motion, moving away from a familiar place to a place unknown. To sustain his journey, the pilgrim brought two things in his sack: bread crumbs to give physical sustenance and the Bible to provide inspiration through the word of God. Drawing on these two sources, the pilgrim fueled his journey.

The body is the place of spiritual deepening. In his quest for constant prayer, the pilgrim was introduced to the hesychast tradition. He learned to pray to Jesus, saying, "Lord Jesus Christ, Son of God, have mercy on me" (PT 60), ideally following the rhythm of his breathing: inhaling at the first invocation, exhaling at the second (PT 83). At first, he painstakingly tracked down the number of invocations until it became second nature to him. The Jesus prayer accompanied the pilgrim throughout his journey, bringing him peace and reminding him of God's constant presence. The experience was one of total prayer that involved the constant rhythm of life in the body, securing a spiritual motion at the heart of daily existence. In him, it is not at the level of any achievement or performance that the body became a place of encounter with the divine but at the very heart of the most essential function: breathing. The body was then the place of personal encounter with and indwelling of God, through the inspiration of the Holy Spirit and the evocation of Christ.

The pilgrim body is also a place of vulnerability and brokenness. The Russian pilgrim's body is perceived as a disabled one. From youth, a weak arm left him unable to perform strenuous manual work. His ability to read and write would compensate for his physical limitations regarding labor. The walking journey generated a physical trial, especially when food was not readily available but also through misfortunes on the journey. Even prayer brought bodily challenges, from the tiredness of reciting a certain number of invocations to the aching induced by the prayer beads. But it would also bring elation and warmth. The asceticism of pilgrimage passes through the body.

The body inhabits spaces. The Russian pilgrim experienced space as a balancing act between the road and the hermitage. The road propels the journey forward but is exposed to risks. The hermitage is the place of deepening. It could take the shape of any simple abode: a garden house, a forester's hut, a churchwarden's lodge. Between the road and the hermitage, a dialectic emerges for the pilgrim body's movement and stability, its exteriority and interiority.

In a discreet way, the body of the pilgrim creates community by its encounters, an ephemeral collective body. With fellow pilgrims journeying on an inner path, a communal body of shared desire is sketched that stretches wide and far, echoing the understanding of the church as a mystical body. The aim of *The Way of a Pilgrim* is to draw the reader also into the collective body of those encountering and hosting the divine on the way.

Pilgrimage as Embodied

The body, and its occupation of space, reminds us that the primary locus of pilgrimage is embodied. Prior to being a metaphor, pilgrimage is movement in a very straightforward, physical sense. Pilgrimages and processions are popular religious phenomena, usually initiated by the desire of the people to reach a particular place to see and touch, and not ideologically constructed. They emerge from the people of God.

Pilgrimage testifies to the sanctification of a place by popular acclaim. Through the incarnation, the sanctity of the human body was underscored, and devotion to the remains of martyrs and saints soon developed. Relics became the focal point of pilgrimages either as parts of human remains or as spaces sanctified by the presence of saints or of Christ himself, in life or through apparitions. The tombs of the apostles in Rome, preserving their remains and the memory of their martyrdom, became early focal points for pilgrimages. Later, the places associated with Christ's life, death, and resurrection in Jerusalem became physical memorials to an embodied divine presence. Most traditional pilgrimage sites claim relics as their core. Since the nineteenth century, however, many major pilgrimage sites grew around places of Marian apparitions, Lourdes and Fatima being the most famous ones. In both instances, the precise location of the apparitions holds a special value in the geography of the shrine.

Hence pilgrimage has a destination, a focal point, a place of ultimate encounter in the flesh by the embodied pilgrim in a space sanctified by the presence of the holy—through Christ, the Virgin Mary, or other saints. The multiplicity of pilgrimage sites in Christianity attests to an understanding of a diffuse holiness undergirding them. Only one is holy, God, but God shares that holiness, his very being, with those receiving him. The places of pilgrimage are memorials to this reflected holiness in the lives of the saints. From an interior perspective, the holiness expressed more visibly in the pilgrimage place opens up the invitation for the pilgrim to share in that holiness, since the divine source is shown as accessible. The pilgrim not only journeys toward a memorial of holiness but is invited to become holy.

Critiques of pilgrimages, from Gregory of Nyssa to the Reformers and beyond, questioned—rightly—pilgrimage from that very perspective of embodiment. Is it necessary to go far to encounter a God who is always near? Isn't it better to use one's resources to take care of neighboring poor through acts of charity? Are some places

Above the open door of a chapel, a tympanum
depicting Mary presenting Jesus invites the Camino
pilgrim to enter. Photo by the author.

more holy than others? Pilgrimages as travels are messy and can
be sources of much sin. Are people really changed by their contact
with holy places? This last question raises the perennial question of
the fruits of pilgrimage: Are pilgrims transformed by their pilgrimage? It is tied to the challenging—and often neglected—question
of the return home. Is the pilgrimage a parenthesis in one's life?
How do concrete fruits last and grow in the pilgrim's life? In *The
Interior Castle*, Saint Teresa of Avila described the inner journey of
the soul with God, only to insist that the growth in love effected
in the journey is to be testified to in works.[7] Hence pilgrimage is not
only physically embodied along the way but also called to produce
an embodied transformation in the pilgrim.

---

7. Teresa of Avila, *The Interior Castle*, 7th Dwelling Place, chap. 4, para. 6, in Kieran
   Kavanaugh and Otilio Rodriguez, eds., *The Collected Works of St. Teresa of Avila*, vol. 2
   (Washington, DC: Institute of Carmelite Studies, 1980), 446.

Eucharist

Jesus embodied a practice of pilgrimage. In the Gospel according to John, readers see him going to Jerusalem for the various festivals (e.g., John 2:23), accomplishing his duty as a faithful Jew. The only mention of the teen Jesus in the canonical Gospels also happens in the context of a family pilgrimage to Jerusalem (Luke 2:41–52). Most importantly, Jesus would spend the last days of his life in Jerusalem on pilgrimage.

Meals are important in the Gospels. Some stretch the boundaries of propriety, reintegrating one into the community (e.g., Zacchaeus in Luke 19:1–10). Others are miraculous, like the feeding of thousands (e.g., John 6:1–14). In preparation for the pilgrim feast of Passover in Jerusalem, Jesus and his disciples shared an important ritual meal. In John's Gospel, prior to the meal, Jesus washed the feet of his disciples (John 13:5–20), a humble task of caring for the bodies of those who were calling him master. By serving them, Jesus showed in deeds the kind of leadership he wanted to see them exercise. During the meal, according to the Synoptic Gospels, he blessed, broke, and shared the bread, saying that it represented his body (e.g., Mark 14:22). He did likewise with the wine, the symbol of his blood, of his life, of a new covenant (Mark 14:23–24). Jesus was heralding a new covenant, a new liberation in this feast of Passover. This paschal meal prefigured the eucharistic celebration.

The Last Supper—with its talk of offered body and poured-out blood—became the entryway to the time in which the preaching of Jesus reached its apex in his body. He was captured, tried, condemned, insulted, flagellated, and put to death on a cross. But he was risen from the dead, with his body showing both discontinuity (people don't recognize him at first, and he can move through closed spaces) and continuity (he can be recognized, he can be touched, and he can prepare food). The body—offered, killed, and risen—is the place where Christian hope is made manifest.

The risen body of Christ did connect with the eucharistic body in the story of the *pèlerins d'Emmaüs* (Emmaus pilgrims), as they are called in French. While they were moving away from Jerusalem at the conclusion of the festival, these disciples were met on the road by the risen Christ, unbeknown to them (Luke 24:13–35). Despite his presence, his explanation of Scriptures, and their burning hearts, it was only at supper at the inn, while he broke the bread, that they recognized him. Realizing the encounter they made, they returned at once to Jerusalem and to the company of the other disciples. The pilgrim encounter through Scriptures and the eucharistic meal became the key to recognizing a radical transformation in their lives and their participation in a larger body—a theme that Paul developed (1 Cor 12:12–31).

The Eucharist is thus at the confluence of the body—offered and shared—the word of God, the holy and risen presence, personal transformation, and community—as a sign of the communal body of Christ. In its praxis, the Eucharist mirrors the pilgrim experience. Along the Camino de Santiago, for me it meant celebration in a foreign language with fellow pilgrims in small churches or at the basilica but also celebration of the Eucharist on a simple table in a park after a good day of walking. At World Youth Day, the enormous Catholic pilgrimage for youth held every two to three years, it also meant to be with more than a million pilgrims of various nations and languages for a celebration of the visible body of Christ. In light of the Jubilee of the year 2000, the reflection on the "tent of the meeting" that the pilgrimage involves entailed not only celebration but also reconciliation and the social commitment to the forgiveness of debt.[8] The mutual recognition of the encounter in pilgrimage led to a desire for celebration, personal change, and social change.

Conclusion

Pilgrimage can be shaped by theological reflection, and theology can learn from the experience of pilgrimage. My intent in this essay is not to saturate the conversation or to offer a comprehensive view of the relationship between pilgrimage and theology but to suggest avenues of reflection through some resonances around journey and body. Pilgrimage teachers and guides could explore with their pilgrims the connection with their tradition or that of their culture. In the case of Christians, some sources of inspiration have been mentioned: the incarnation, the collective dimension at work in the biblical sources of pilgrimage or in the Eucharist, and the importance of memory and narrative. The dynamic between interiority and exteriority, as seen in the involvement of the body in prayer and the inner quest of the Russian pilgrim, offers a helpful lens to read one's experience of pilgrimage. The looming question of the transformation through pilgrimage is also important. The recourse to theological reflection can enhance and deepen the pilgrim's journey.

---

8. See Pontifical Council for the Pastoral Care of Migrants and Itinerant People, "The Pilgrimage in the Great Jubilee," Vatican, April 25, 1998, https://www.vatican.va/roman _curia/pontifical_councils/migrants/documents/rc_pc_migrants_doc_19980425 _pilgrimage_en.htm.

Questions for Reflection

1. Pilgrimages come in various shapes and forms. What connections could you draw between your own actual—or intended—experience(s) of pilgrimage and some dimensions of the Jewish and Christian biblical tradition related to pilgrimage?
2. What is the aim or destination of your pilgrimage? How would you articulate the way and the destination?
3. How would you ascertain the personal and the collective dimension of pilgrimage?
4. Pilgrimage is embodied—even seen as a spiritual metaphor. It means it is lived in the body—with its strengths and challenges—but it also calls the pilgrim to change and transform. How could one foster a greater embodiment in pilgrimage and its aftermath?
5. Memory is an important component of pilgrimage. Which collective memories participate in your pilgrimage? How would you memorialize your pilgrimage (diary, pictures, etc.)?

Select Annotated Bibliography

Bartholomew, Craig, and Fred Hughes, eds. *Explorations in a Christian Theology of Pilgrimage*. Hants: Ashgate, 2004.
    An edited book covering a wide range of theological issues around pilgrimage from the biblical, historical, and theological perspectives, with insightful essays.
Brouillette, André. *The Pilgrim Paradigm: Faith in Motion*. Mahwah, NJ: Paulist Press, 2021.

A monograph on the theology of pilgrimage through the lens of a phenomenology of pilgrimage, its biblical resonances, its modern use for identity in the *Testament* of Ignatius of Loyola, and the "Pilgrim Church" ethos post–Vatican II.

Ignatius of Loyola. *A Pilgrim's Testament: The Memoirs of Saint Ignatius of Loyola*. Edited by Barton T. Geger, SJ. Boston: Institute of Jesuit Sources, 2020.

A concise narrative of the life of the great Spanish saint and founder of the Society of Jesus, in which he used the moniker of "pilgrim." This life pilgrimage led him first to Jerusalem (and back!) but eventually to studies, priesthood, and mission in Rome.

Pentkovsky, Aleksei, ed. *The Pilgrim's Tale*. New York: Paulist Press, 1999.

A nineteenth-century Russian Orthodox spiritual classic featuring a wandering pilgrim on a quest for constant prayer who crosses the path of a variety of characters.

Pontifical Council for the Pastoral Care of Migrants and Itinerant People. "The Pilgrimage in the Great Jubilee." Vatican, April 25, 1998. https://www.vatican.va/roman_curia/pontifical _councils/migrants/documents/rc_pc_migrants_doc_19980425 _pilgrimage_en.htm.

———. "The Shrine: Memory, Presence and Prophecy of the Living God." Vatican, May 8, 1999. https://www.vatican.va/ roman_curia/pontifical_councils/ migrants/documents/rc_pc_migrants_doc_19990525 _shrine_en.html.

Theological documents written by the Holy See (Vatican) in preparation for the Jubilee of 2000. They offer a broad and cogent reflection on the theme of pilgrimage and the shrine as its destination in the Christian tradition.

Walton, Heather. "Theological Perspectives on Christian Pilgrimage." In *Christian Pilgrimage, Landscape and Heritage: Journeying to the Sacred*, by Avril Maddrell, Veronica della Dora, Alessandro Scafi, and Heather Walton, 22–40. New York: Routledge, 2015.

A concise presentation of important aspects of the theological reflection on pilgrimage according to various branches of Christianity.

Chapter 3

The Pilgrim in a Developmental Context and Pilgrimage as a Developmental Experience

A Psychological Lens

Heather A. Warfield
Antioch University

Pilgrims bring to their journeys an array of past experiences, meanings, identities, and expectations. Pilgrims are also at varying stages of development, and the pilgrimage occurs within the larger life narrative rather than separate from it. Pilgrimage guides and teachers may create more meaningful experiences by considering models of human development and the pilgrim within such frameworks. In addition to positioning the pilgrim within a developmental paradigm, the pilgrimage itself may be envisaged as a particular developmental process within the context of the pilgrim's general growth and development as a human. Based on my phenomenological research on pilgrims' experiences, I have learned that pilgrimages can be significant experiences for pilgrims and that the learning and transformation begin long before the actual journey and end well after the conclusion of the travel. As such, pilgrimage guides and teachers can integrate the knowledge of the stages into the facilitation of more meaningful experiences for pilgrims.

For the sake of brevity, I focus my attention in this chapter on the developmental period of young adulthood, and the developmental models I selected reflect a young adulthood stage. The chapter is intended not as an in-depth review of developmental theories but as a cursory overview of some of the models relevant to young adult pilgrims. The second part of the chapter is intended to map out the particular developmental process of a pilgrimage journey.

Part A: Young Adult Pilgrims and Developmental Considerations

Stage models of psychological development emerged in the early twentieth century as an extension of the Darwinian (1859) theory of biological evolution in the nineteenth century. Underpinning both evolutionary and developmental models of growth and development are the notions that (a) growth occurs over time and (b) one stage or level builds upon the previous level. When applied to human psychological development, we accept that humans progress through psychological stages of growth or development, which have approximate parallels to chronological aging. People at various stages of human development go on pilgrimage journeys, often during transitional points (or rites of passage) as they pass from one stage to another. The liminality of the pilgrimage journey can parallel the liminal space of leaving one stage of development and not yet reaching the next.

Alexandria Egler notes the importance of the outer and inner journeys as significant contributors to the learning and transformation that result from a pilgrimage. It is the inner, psychological journey that remains the focus of this chapter.[1] As this book is envisaged for pilgrimage teachers and guides, it is likely that many

---

1. Alexandria Egler, "Pilgrimage as Religiously Educative," in *Pilgrimage as Transformative Process*, ed. Heather A. Warfield and Kate Hetherington (Leiden, Netherlands: Brill, 2018), 23–32.

of the accompanying pilgrims will be students and young adults. As such, I have selected five theories of human development with a focus on the chronological era of young adulthood. *Of note is that these models of development are not without criticism and limitations; however, a critical analysis of the models is beyond the scope of this chapter. Additionally, these models and stages may not be relevant to all pilgrims and are included here as a launch point for consideration.*

There are dozens of theories of human development, and I have selected five of the most historically relevant theories through which to explore how a pilgrimage journey may result in learning for young adults. In case the reader is unfamiliar with these theories, a summary of each follows. Sigmund Freud posited that humans progress through psychosexual stages of development that span from infancy to adulthood.[2] These stages include the oral stage (birth to age one), anal stage (ages one to three), phallic stage (ages three to six), latent stage (age six to puberty), and genital stage (puberty to death). Each stage is focused on an erogenous zone and the mastery of a task in order to progress to the next stage. For example, toilet training is the task for the anal stage of development. Erik Erikson expanded on Freud's ideas and asserted there are eight stages of psychosocial development through which humans pass.[3] At each stage, a conflict or "crisis" arises, and a psychological quality or ego strength emerges. If the crisis is not adequately addressed, the person remains stagnated. The stages are binary and include trust versus mistrust (birth to eighteen months), autonomy versus shame and doubt (eighteen months to three years), initiative versus guilt (ages three to five), industry versus inferiority (ages five to thirteen), identity versus role confusion (ages thirteen to twenty-one), intimacy versus isolation (ages twenty-one to thirty-nine), generativity versus stagnation (ages

---

2. Sigmund Freud, *Three Contributions to the Theory of Sexuality* (New York: Nervous and Mental Disease Publishing, 1905).

3. See Erik Erikson, *Identity and the Life Cycle* (New York: W. W. Norton, 1959).

forty to sixty-five), and ego integrity versus despair (ages sixty-five and older). The theory was expanded to include a ninth stage conceptualized by Joan Erikson in 1998 as the "woven cycle of life."[4]

Lawrence Kohlberg explicated a theory of moral development that consists of three levels with two stages each.[5] Birth to age nine includes the first stage of obedience and punishment orientation and the second stage of individualism and exchange. Stage three is the good boy / nice girl orientation, and stage four is the law and order orientation. Level three includes stage five, social contract orientation, and stage six, universal ethical principles. Each stage is focused on the development of moral reasoning and moves from rigid "good/bad" to abstract reasoning. Jean Piaget explored four stages of intellectual or cognitive development. The stages include sensorimotor (birth to eighteen through twenty-four months), preoperational (ages two to seven), concrete operational (ages seven to eleven), and formal operational (adolescence to adulthood).[6] Each stage has characteristics and goals that progress from the previous stage, and the focus is on how humans acquire knowledge and intelligence. James Fowler broadened the developmental paradigm to include stages of faith development.[7] He proposed that people progress through six stages in their faith journey. These include intuitive-projective faith, mythical-literal faith, synthetic-conventional faith, individuative-reflective faith, conjunctive faith, and universalizing faith.

Table 1 depicts the five models of human development, with a focus on the young adult stage of each model.

---

4. See Joan Erikson and Erik Erikson, *The Life Cycle Completed* (New York: W. W. Norton, 1998).

5. See Lawrence Kohlberg, *Moral Development: Kohlberg's Original Study of Moral Development* (New York: Taylor and Francis, 1994).

6. See Jean Piaget and Bärbel Inhelder, *The Psychology of the Child* (New York: Basic, 1969).

7. James W. Fowler, *Stages of Faith: The Psychology of Human Development and the Quest for Meaning* (New York: HarperCollins, 1981).

Table 1: Young adult development and pilgrimage

Theory	Stage	Stage description	Pilgrimage considerations
Psychosexual development[1]	Stage 5: Genital	Experimenting sexually and relationally.	Interacting with others as sexual beings, forming significant attachments with others, and exploring sexuality and sexual identity.
Psychosocial development[2]	Stage 6: Intimacy vs. isolation	Exploring relationships, making commitments to others, and forming strong intimate partnerships.	Self-exploration, building mature platonic/romantic relationships, taking emotional risks.
Moral development[3]	Stage 4: Law and order orientation	Accepting social norms related to what is good and moral and internalizing moral standards learned from role models. There is an emphasis on living up to societal expectations. People in this stage also begin to consider all of society when making moral decisions.	Learning about the "Other," questioning moral absolutes, considering the individual in the context of the group, managing paradox, and thinking about laws vs. individual moral codes.
Faith development[4]	Stage 4: Individuative-reflective faith	Taking personal responsibility for spiritual beliefs and feelings. Beliefs and practices can take on more complexity, and the person gains a sense of tolerance and open-mindedness.	Strengthening of faith and recognizing that others may have a different faith, which does not diminish one's own faith. Considering people and events through more complex spiritual frameworks.
Cognitive development[5]	Stage 4: Formal operational	Thinking becomes more complex, and systematic planning and goals become achievable. People can consider hypothetical ideas and consider "what if?"	Considering abstract concepts and reflecting on moral absolutism vs. situational decision-making.

1. Freud, *Three Contributions*.
2. Erikson, *Identity and the Life Cycle*.
3. Kohlberg, *Moral Development*.
4. Fowler, *Stages of Faith*.
5. Piaget and Inhelder, *Psychology of the Child*.

Pilgrimage provides the time and space for internal and external growth and learning. From a psychosexual paradigm, the pilgrimage experience may provide the opportunity for building intimate relationships, exploring sexual identity, and relating to others in new ways. For example, I recently completed qualitative interviews with LGBTQ+ individuals who went on a pilgrimage journey as part of their sexual identity development. One theme that emerged is that the pilgrimage provided a context for "trying on" one's identity before a formal "coming out" to friends and family. Knowledge of this can be important for pilgrimage guides, as members of their pilgrimage groups may be in similar situations.

Like the focus of the genital stage in the psychosexual model, from a psychosocial lens, pilgrims may be in a stage wherein they are learning to navigate significant intimate relationship milestones. A pilgrimage provides the opportunity for learning about how to relate to others, how to be vulnerable with others, and how to be honest about one's relational needs. Like "trying on" one's sexual identity, many pilgrims find pilgrimage journeys provide meaningful contexts for authenticity and building deep relationships. Often, the intimate conversations lead to a sense of a new "pilgrim family" construct. Further, the communication skills developed on the pilgrimage remain after the pilgrim returns home. And many a pilgrim has met a long-term partner or spouse on a pilgrimage.

From a moral development paradigm, the pilgrimage provides an opportunity for one to consider laws and moral codes, especially if one is interacting with others from different countries. A pilgrim can spend time pondering whether people are different or whether we are all members of a large human family. Another important consideration is that the pilgrimage can be the first time a young adult is presented with paradoxical dilemmas, and there is an opportunity for growth as pilgrims learn to balance many truths at the same time. For example, one might meet a pilgrim who has a criminal record, and this is shared during the course of conversation. The young adult may grapple with the notion that this person can be both a criminal and a unique person with compassion and difficult life circumstances.

While faith development may not be relevant to all pilgrims, I note it because it applies to many. A young adult in the individuative-reflective stage begins to take responsibility for spiritual beliefs and practices. In addition, a person is able to hold these beliefs and practices while also not being threatened by another person's beliefs and practices. There is an ability to manage many truths at one time. Relevant to pilgrimage is that a pilgrim in this stage may have established beliefs, be able to articulate these, and accept truths from another person. In some instances, the pilgrimage may lead to a new or reinvigorated faith, and the pilgrim may start at the beginning stage of faith development. This first stage may be marked with internalized spiritual experiences that are gained from the pilgrimage environment rather than from within.

From a cognitive development perspective, a young adult can manage more complex, and often competing, thoughts and ideas. The pilgrimage will certainly provide opportunities for the consideration of paradox and critical thinking. Additionally, a person in this stage is able to formulate long-term plans that take into consideration many variables. The pilgrimage experience may provide the environment for changes in areas such as academic study, career, and relationships. Internal thoughts about these life domains will likely occur, and the interpersonal encounters with other pilgrims will provide additional opportunities for consideration.

Part B: Developmental Stages of the Pilgrimage Process

This part of the chapter considers pilgrimage as its own developmental process with subprocesses related to transformation, healing, identity development, and learning. These processes begin long before the journey commences and continue long after the journey ends. The stages of the pilgrimage process are delineated, and the learning considerations for each stage are explored. In many ways, the stage model I have presented is as much about pilgrim identity development as it is about learning, and I hope to explore this identity development in more depth in a later publication. Inherent in this stage model is the recognition that not all journeys are pilgrimages and not all travelers are pilgrims. Furthermore, not all those who go on pilgrimages self-identify as pilgrims. Thus the model is intended as a framework for (a) self-identified pilgrims and (b) journeys that one identifies as pilgrimages.

Pilgrimage journeys can be intentional (e.g., a well-planned experience) or unintentional (e.g., a journey that one labels a pilgrimage after the fact). Both of these types of pilgrimages follow a similar developmental process in that there is a beginning, middle, and end to the journey. However, for the sake of this chapter, I will address the pilgrimage that is intentional, as this is likely the type of journey for which this manual will be utilized. Furthermore, an intentional journey will yield far more significant opportunities for learning and reflection than journeys that are unintentional.

As with the developmental models previously discussed, each stage of the pilgrimage process builds upon the previous stage. The eight stages of the process are (1) decision to embark on the pilgrimage, (2) preparation for the journey, (3) journey, (4) entering sacred space, (5) experience at the site, (6) completion of the pilgrimage / return, (7) reintegration, and (8) integration of the pilgrimage experience. The stages are fully described below.

Stage 1: Decision to Embark on the Pilgrimage

The first stage of the pilgrimage process commences when the pilgrim commits to making a meaningful journey to a sacred place. From this point forward, each activity related to the journey becomes part of the pilgrimage. In many cases, pilgrims have been contemplating a pilgrimage journey for many years. For adherents to religions such as Islam, the pilgrimage (hajj) journey is a fundamental part of religious practice (one of the five pillars of Islam), and the pilgrim has likely planned for decades to embark on the journey. At this stage, the journey unfolds in the mind and begins to manifest outside of the mind. Pilgrims tell others about their plans, they conceptualize the time frame in which the journey will occur, and they begin to turn their gaze toward the pilgrimage and away from the routine. This pivot away from the routine marks the beginning of the liminal phase, in which the pilgrim disembarks mentally from the social and relational constructs that encapsulated them to this point. From a relational perspective, tension may begin to emerge, as the pilgrim may be viewed as pulling away from partners, family, and friends as the pilgrim identity emerges. Those around the pilgrim may not understand the need or desire (or even call) to go on the pilgrimage and may display various forms of resistance to the journey and the sacrifices (e.g., time and money) needed for the experience. At this stage, the pilgrim may start learning about the contextual setting for the pilgrimage (i.e., geography, culture, weather, customs, language). Additionally, the pilgrim may start learning about what it means to be a pilgrim for this particular journey. If the pilgrim is embarking on a pilgrimage that is outside of their familial or social structure, a process of differentiation may occur. If the pilgrimage is congruent with their familial or social structure, the pilgrim may start to experience an elevated status within the structure. There may be a sense of euphoria that the journey is happening or a sense of apprehension as the unknown details of the pilgrimage rise to the fore. For pilgrimages such as the hajj, there are contractual details that emerge as the pilgrim enters a financial arrangement with an approved tour company. The learning at this stage is primarily based on prior knowledge, expectations, and planning, and this stage can be considered the apex of experiences up to this point. It is also important to note that pilgrims may make the decision to go on a pilgrimage as the result of a life crisis, such as the end of a relationship or the death of a loved one, or as an attempt to find healing when other methods have failed. Thus the decision itself represents a sense of control over one's destiny, which can lead to a sense of empowerment and agency about one's life.

Stage 2: Preparation for the Journey

The activities that characterize the second stage, preparation for the journey, take on a "separation from normal life" pattern, such as training for long-distance walking, preparing to leave one's family or surroundings, obtaining a visa, and arranging for time away from work or other regular responsibilities. This stage may last days, months, or even years depending on the circumstances and specific religious construct of the pilgrimage. Other preparatory rites may include altering one's physical appearance through shaving the head and eyebrows, ritual bathing, applying perfumes, and fasting from food, drink, or sexual relations. Because of the varied length of time of the preparation stage, pilgrims may experience it as a time of intense learning. Pilgrims typically dedicate long periods of time to gathering information about the pilgrimage route/rituals, reading about the experiences of previous pilgrims, and devoting mental energy to imagining the journey. The social milieu also expands to others who self-identify as pilgrims. If the community of pilgrims cannot be found in the same geographical location, online communities emerge as important sources of support. Often, pilgrims join Facebook groups focused on a particular pilgrimage or other types of online discussion forums in which members share stories and logistical information with the group. From an identity development perspective, identity fusion begins to emerge as the personal pilgrim identity merges with the social group of other pilgrims. The pilgrim now experiences membership in and acceptance by the community of pilgrims.

Stage 3: Journey

The third stage of the pilgrimage process is the actual journey along a route and/or to a sacred space. This stage can last hours, days, weeks, or months and includes all outer experiences, such as travel, movement, interacting with others, sleeping in new places, and so on. Along the path, pilgrims may gather evidence of the journey, such as some type of credential or pictures of specific places along the journey (such as the stations of the Via Delarosa in Jerusalem). The third stage also includes the inner experiences of the pilgrim. These can include self-reflection, telling and retelling one's life story in the mind, contemplating relationships, grieving, and existential questioning. The internal processes at this stage are varied and individualized. There is an interplay among one's private thoughts, interactions with other pilgrims, interactions with local hosts, and experiences in the natural world. Inner and outer learning are expansive. For example, the pilgrim can learn about a new culture, language, and customs. One may encounter pilgrims from many locations throughout the globe. These interactions may lead to an important challenging of preferences and ideologies. Communal meals provide further opportunities for intimate conversations about one's life experiences, expectations, and plans for the future. The pilgrim may start to question long-held assumptions about the self, others, and the world. In terms of learning theory, this stage aligns with Jack Mezirow's disorienting dilemma wherein the learner is launched into a transformative learning process.[8]

Stage 4: Entering the Sacred Space

The fourth stage is the final preparation to enter the sacred space. The sacred space is that which is the focal point of the pilgrimage (e.g., the Cathedral of Saint James, Mont Saint-Michel, or the Ka'bah). This stage may be viewed as a "pilgrimage within a pilgrimage." All preparations and intentions have been focused on reaching this space. Pilgrims may form organized processions, chant mantras, or engage in a specific ritual that highlights the separation of this activity from everyday life. Following the rituals, pilgrims often become silent, remove their shoes, keep their faces focused on the shrine or sacred space, and clasp their hands as a sign of reverence. Despite being surrounded by other pilgrims, the pilgrim retreats into the self.

Stage 5: Experience at Sacred Site

The fifth step of the pilgrimage is the actual experience at the sacred site. This stage is characterized by behaviors such as placing offerings, performing the appropriate type of worship (with sound or without), ringing bells, touching a part of the sacred space, weeping, kissing the sacred object, praying in front of the image, or placing an

---

8. Jack Mezirow, "An Overview of Transformative Learning," in *Contemporary Theories of Learning*, ed. Knud Illeris, 90–105 (London: Routledge, 2009).

object at a shrine. The prepilgrimage meaning and expectations are met with the reality of the "here and now" sensory experience. Pilgrims may encounter a variety of emotions, including being elated, awestruck, or euphoric. However, it is also possible that pilgrims may encounter disappointment, a sense of being underwhelmed, or frustration if the experience does not match the expectation. As a result, cognitive dissonance may be experienced by the pilgrim. Cognitive dissonance is the mental discomfort experienced when one encounters conflicting beliefs, values, attitudes, or behaviors. This may emerge as anxiety, shame, regret, or stress. To alleviate the internal discomfort, pilgrims may express to the group that their experiences were more positive than they actually were.

Stage 6: Completion of Pilgrimage / Return
The sixth step of the pilgrimage is focused on the completion of the journey and the return home to one's familiar surroundings. Additionally, tourist activities may take predominance at this stage, and pilgrims may engage in various local customs and events. Because of the local economic impact of a pilgrimage site, there are often a variety of activities to be experienced by the pilgrim at the conclusion of the sacred journey.[9] At this stage, pilgrims may be relieved, proud, and fulfilled. However, many pilgrims may begin to feel a sense of loss as they transition from being on the pilgrimage to returning to a life of routine. Some may extend their travels for a few extra days in order to remain in the pilgrimage space. Pilgrims may be apprehensive about returning to loved ones who may not understand or be interested in the pilgrims' experiences. Additionally, many pilgrims have connected in meaningful ways with other pilgrims and may feel dismissed and frustrated at the lack of

---

9. See Linda Davidson and David M. Gitlitz, *Pilgrimage from the Ganges to Graceland: An Encyclopedia* (Santa Barbara, CA: ABC-CLIO, 2002).

intensity and vulnerability of conversations with loved ones. During the pilgrimage, a pilgrim may have decided to change careers, pursue academic endeavors, or end a relationship. The implications of such decisions begin to emerge as the pilgrim returns to the prepilgrimage environment.

Stage 7: Reintegration

The seventh stage of the pilgrimage process is reintegrating with one's routine environment. Pilgrims returning to their prepilgrimage construct often report feeling discomfort because an internal transformation has occurred for them, but the people at home have remained the same. Following from the sixth stage, pilgrims may have a profound sense of grief related to missing life during the pilgrimage. The duration of the pilgrimage is certainly a factor in terms of the depth of angst related to reintegration. For pilgrims who have engaged in a weeks-long or months-long pilgrimage, the reintegration can be more challenging. Regardless of the duration, there is a period of time when the pilgrim must readjust to the prepilgrimage context.

Stage 8: Integration of Pilgrimage Experience

This stage may last from the months following the pilgrimage up to the rest of one's life. One's life narrative now includes identifying oneself as a pilgrim. This may have various representations based on culture. It may include a status change, such as becoming a "hajji" after completing the hajj. People may join groups associated with the pilgrim identity, such as the American Pilgrims on the Camino organization. Pilgrims may begin to display outward indicators of the pilgrimage—displaying holy water, wearing a pilgrimage medallion, or getting a tattoo. During this phase, the pilgrim may actively plan another pilgrimage. Relationships may form around the pilgrim identity, and the prepilgrimage relational and social constructs may not be congruent. Pilgrims may continue to associate with other pilgrims and attend events that "keep the pilgrimage alive." Other outward signs, such as referencing the pilgrim identity, can be observed. Pilgrimage may be adopted as a metaphor for life or other challenging scenarios. Pilgrims feel a connection to other pilgrims and a sense of shared experience despite differences in specificity of pilgrimage journeys. Travel may take on a more sacred intention, and future travel may be framed from a pilgrimage paradigm.

Recommendations for Pilgrimage Guides and Teachers

Pilgrimage can be a holistic and transformational learning endeavor as well as a self-contained therapeutic intervention.[10] Because the pilgrimage can be such a momentous experience for many people, guides who have a basic understanding of developmental frameworks will be in a better position to understand the pilgrims in their groups as well as to contribute to the growth and learning of the pilgrims. The developmental models outlined above are intended as a starting place, and the reader is invited to explore other developmental paradigms.

In terms of pilgrimage being a developmental process, certainly the journey itself is transformational; however, it is important to acknowledge that the journey begins long before the travel and ends long after the return home. An intentional focus on the inner processes of the pilgrim before and after the journey can lead to a more

---

10. Heather A. Warfield, "From Existential to Ideological Communitas: Can Pilgrimage Connect and Transform the World?," in *Pilgrimage as Transformative Process*, ed. Heather A. Warfield and Kate Hetherington (Leiden, Netherlands: Brill, 2018), 33–42.

Pilgrimage to the Cathédrale Notre-Dame
de Reims, 2021. Photo by author.

robust pilgrimage experience. For pilgrimage guides and leaders, it is important to recognize that pilgrims bring to the experience wide-ranging beliefs, values, expectations, and meanings. As such, guides can create a platform for exploration before the pilgrimage journey to facilitate self-reflection. It can be helpful to explore the motivations for the journey, what the pilgrim hopes will result from it, and the expectations for what may be experienced. It can also be helpful to discuss previous situations wherein the pilgrim experienced a scenario where expectation did not meet reality. In particular, scenarios wherein sensory expectations and experiences have been incongruent can lead to expectation management. For example, pilgrims may expect that a journey or sacred place may feel, smell, or be experienced in a specific manner, and the reality may be different. This incongruence can lead to the sense that the pilgrimage is not valid, when in fact the pilgrimage or site itself exists independently of the pilgrim. A recognition of this fact reminds the pilgrim that the pilgrimage is intended to transform the pilgrim rather than the pilgrim controlling the pilgrimage.

Guides and teachers may wish to implement focused activities during the preparation and return stages of the pilgrimage. The journey itself likely has a particular focus, and the learning can be enhanced by attending to these other stages. An example might be facilitating in-person or virtual preparation groups or classes. Pilgrims can explore motivations for their pilgrimages, their worldviews, their biases about pilgrimage, their culture, "the Other," and their expectations for the journey. This type of forum can also provide a space for pilgrims who may encounter relational and/or social challenges related to time and space away from loved ones. There are adequate resources related to the practical minutia of pilgrimage journeys (e.g., clothing, equipment, travel logistics) but not to the psychological dynamics of the pilgrimage experience.

Any opportunity for self-reflection and discussion about diversity of expectations and life experiences will help facilitate learning for the pilgrim. The time following the pilgrimage can be critical for the cultivation of additional learning. Providing spaces for pilgrims to honestly discuss their experiences will result in pilgrims being able to shape their pilgrimage narratives, share their experiences with others, and continue to engage in a pilgrimage community. As noted by Schnell and Pali, pilgrims reported greater meaning in their lives four months following the end of the pilgrimage.[11] As a result, postpilgrimage forums or gatherings can continue several months after the pilgrimage. Pilgrimage journeys abound with learning opportunities. Learning about the self, others, cultures, customs, and spiritual practices can occur before, during, and after a pilgrimage. A pilgrimage teacher or guide is in an excellent position to help facilitate learning and meaning for the pilgrim, and knowledge about human development and the stages of the pilgrimage process offer tools for learning cultivation.

Questions for Reflection

1. In terms of human development models, which model may be useful for a contextual understanding of yourself or your group of pilgrims?
2. As a guide or teacher, how is your own development and identity impacted by leading others on a pilgrimage journey?
3. How different is it to engage in a pilgrimage as a guide versus solely as a pilgrim?

---

11. Tatjana Schnell and Sarah Pali, "Pilgrimage Today: The Meaning-Making Potential of Ritual," *Mental Health, Religion, and Culture* 16, no. 9 (2013): 887–902.

4. During the preparation stage, what additional information and/or activities may be helpful to position the pilgrimage in the greater life narrative of the pilgrim?
5. How can pilgrim expectations be realistically addressed? What about when pilgrimages lead to unintended outcomes or are incongruent with expectations?
6. How can long-term reflection and integration of the pilgrimage experience be facilitated?

Select Annotated Bibliography

Cousineau, Phil. *The Art of Pilgrimage: The Seeker's Guide to Making Travel Sacred*. Berkeley, CA: Conari, 2012.
> Cousineau offers an accessible conceptualization of pilgrimages as meaningful journeys and the importance of intention in creating these travel endeavors.

Di Giovine, Michael A., and Jayeon Choe, eds. *Pilgrimage beyond the Officially Sacred: Understanding the Geographies of Religion and Spirituality in Sacred Travel*. New York: Routledge, 2020.
> The editors of this book engage the questions of who and what sanctions a pilgrimage. They move the argument beyond a religious definition of pilgrimage and challenge the reader to consider an expansion of what constitutes a pilgrimage journey.

Dubisch, Jill, and Michael Winkleman, eds. *Pilgrimage and Healing*. Tucson: University of Arizona Press, 2014.
> This edited volume provides a critical connection between medical anthropology and psychology with an emphasis on the whole(ing) that can occur from a pilgrimage.

Schnell, Tatjana, and Sarah Pali. "Pilgrimage Today: The Meaning-Making Potential of Ritual." *Mental Health, Religion, and Culture* 16, no. 9 (2013): 887–902.

The authors provide data demonstrating that pilgrimages lead to greater meaning during and after the journey.

Warfield, Heather A., ed. *Multidisciplinary Perspectives on Pilgrimage: Historical, Current, and Future Directions*. Oxford: Peter Lang, 2022.

This edited book examines pilgrimage phenomena from a spectrum of academic disciplines and fields of study. Each chapter contains literature, theoretical perspectives, research methodologies, and recommendations from fourteen distinct academic disciplines/fields of study. The volume would be useful for guided pilgrimage experiences in which students and faculty may be from varied disciplinary backgrounds and the faculty/guides wish to create shared knowledge among the group.

Warfield, Heather A., and Kate Hetherington, eds. *Pilgrimage as Transformative Process*. Leiden, Netherlands: Brill, 2018.

This edited volume links the many types of transformation that occur before, during, and after a pilgrimage journey. Several chapters focus on the educational outcomes of faculty-led pilgrimages.

Chapter 4

Art as Pilgrimage, Pilgrimage as Art

Kathryn R. Barush and Hung Pham, SJ

Graduate Theological Union, Berkeley and the Office of Ignatian Spirituality, UCS Central South Province

The idea of pilgrimage as pedagogy assumes an embodied and contextual approach. This chapter explores art and visual culture as an integral part of the spiritual practice of pilgrimage. It suggests some strategies for engaging art-making as a preparation for pilgrimage, describes ways that sacred art and material culture as experienced along the Camino Ignaciano can be a powerful means to experience history and engender a sense of divine presence, and argues for the importance of art, either created or collected, as a souvenir—a way for students to recall and to share their pilgrimage experiences. These three themes are interrelated. Such objects served throughout history, and still serve, both as proof that the pilgrim had visited the place and as a physical manifestation of the spirit—or, in Jas Elsner and Simon Coleman's words, the "charisma" of the sacred center: "In this way, the sacred landscape becomes diffused, permeating even the everyday lives of those who have never been to the site itself."[1]

---

1. Simon Coleman and John Elsner, *Pilgrimage: Past and Present in the World Religions* (Cambridge, MA: Harvard University Press, 1995), 6. See also James R. Blaettler, SJ, "Through Emmaus Eyes: Art, Liturgy and Monastic Ideology at Santo Domingo de Silos" (PhD diss., University of Chicago, 1989), which describes the twelfth-century "exsilensis" (Silos) monks, who were as pilgrims en route spiritually reminded by a

Our 2015 pilgrimage along the Camino Ignaciano in Spain, which was embedded in a class on Ignatian spirituality, will function as a primary case study, but reference will also be given to subsequent courses taught and retreats led after the Covid-19 pandemic—and how these themes and ideas have continued to resonate.

Art can inspire pilgrimages, become a pedagogical tool along the way, and serve as a powerful aide-mémoire of a transformative experience. This is a wide-reaching topic, and the type and scope of art and objects encountered will differ from pilgrimage to pilgrimage, from culture to culture, from religious tradition to religious tradition. That being said, the critical frameworks and pedagogical approaches that we employed can be used across a number of contexts. Kathryn Barush has engaged these pedagogical tools and techniques in courses that she has developed and taught in the ecumenical and interreligious context of the Graduate Theological Union (GTU) in Berkeley, California. These applications have included courses on art and pilgrimage, Marian art in global contexts, and (starting in spring 2020, as the Covid-19 pandemic struck and pilgrimages were curtailed), virtual sacred spaces. Hung Pham has since adapted the Camino course into various virtual pilgrimages during the Covid-19 pandemic for Kansas City and Singapore, as well as an upcoming Camino for different groups of the Ignatian family.

Art-Making in Preparation for Pilgrimage

Art-making can be a way for student pilgrims to both mediate and record an experience of pilgrimage, but it can also be a formative part of the preparation process. For the duration of the spring semester and then for two weeks in the summer of 2015, Pham and

---

relief sculpture of the nearby Way to Santiago de Compostela and the steady path of visitors to the local grave of their founder.

Barush, in collaboration with Josep Lluís Iriberri, SJ, director of Oficina del Peregrino del Camino Ignaciano, led a group of twelve graduate students in the Camino Ignaciano course at the Jesuit School of Theology of Santa Clara University in Berkeley (hereafter JST), which is a member school of the GTU. Envisioning the students as pilgrims and the classroom as a road, the course emphasized the importance of encountering sacred space and objects in situ and doing theology in the context of a Camino. We engaged with Ignatius's use of pilgrimage metaphors and motifs throughout the *Autobiography* and the *Spiritual Exercises* and his emphasis on active embodiment through engaging with religious objects, sacred spaces, and the environment, all of which were integral to his process of formation. It was the conjunction of journey and metaphor that Ignatius engages throughout the *Spiritual Exercises* that became our pedagogical framework. Like Ignatius, the Camino served as a "composition of place" where the encounter with the divine remained alive and active in each step of the journey. Our experience traveling 250 or so miles with the students across Spain engendered this kind of encounter and resonated with the conjunction of pilgrimage metaphor and praxis.

Saint Ignatius of Loyola (1491–1556) considered the crucial interplay between physical journey and contemplation in his *Spiritual Exercises*, a foundational text for the religious order he cofounded in the sixteenth century, now known as the Society of Jesus. In the vision of Ignatius, the modern Jesuits seek to be in union with God in all things or to be "contemplatives in action," laboring on behalf of global justice, peace, and dialogue.[2] His own spiritual journey was informed, in part, by encounters with art and

---

2. See, for example, "About Us," Jesuits.org, accessed October 28, 2020, https://www .jesuits.org/about-us/the-jesuits/, and the mission "to work for reconciliation every day—with God, with human beings, and with the environment."

objects that acted as powerful adjuncts to prayer and were instrumental in his development of the idea of "composition of place," a hallmark of Ignatian spirituality.

After being struck by a cannonball at the Battle of Pamplona, which had shattered his legs and necessitated a long and painful recovery, Ignatius committed his life to the pursuit of holiness through imitating the lives of the saints and walking in the footsteps of Christ in perpetual penance.[3] From Loyola, Ignatius (then still called Íñigo) made a foot pilgrimage through Aránzazu, Montserrat, and Manresa before entering Jerusalem on September 4, 1523, spending nearly one-and-a-half years on the road. Trading his sword and knightly clothes for the simple garments of the pious pilgrim, Ignatius slowly learned not to run ahead but to open himself to be led by the Spirit. Step by step, a camino—a road—was opened, leading him to ever deeper conversion and transformation.[4] As a *peregrino* (pilgrim), each of the physical locations and spaces through which he journeyed became an entry point into the transformative process of his interior life. Thus, what took place on the physical level was reflected in the depth of the inward journey of his soul.

In preparation for the pilgrimage, we engaged in not just reading about Ignatius but, as Ignatius had inspired us to do, also reflecting on how the Spirit had been actively laboring in each of our own life journeys, through the mapping and narrating of our own autobiographies both visually and verbally. In doing so, we walked together as Ignatian "companions." One of the in-class activities that we participated in as a group was creating small mandala-like drawings on shrinkable plastic that visually embodied our personal journeys

---

3. Ignatius, *Saint Ignatius of Loyola: Personal Writings*, trans. J. A. Munitiz and P. Endean (London: Penguin, 1996), 12.
4. J. Nadal, "Dialogi pro Societate," *Fontes Narrativi de S. Ignatio de Loyola, Monumenta Historica Societatis Iesu*, vol. 2, ed. Candidus de Dalmases (Rome: Monumenta Historica Societatis Iesu, 1951), 228.

up to that point. While no prior art experience was required, after having reflected on their life journeys up until this point, students discerned and opted for colors that spoke to their personalities, meditated on patterns that mirrored their life paths, and elected to use symbols that highlighted their experience as part of a guided retreat–like activity. Art-making became a pilgrimage in and of itself, and the finished products engendered a journey with their circular, spiral-like designs and nested circles of meaningful iconographic patterns and forms.

Once the design was created using colored pencils, the product was heated in a toaster oven, where it thickened and was sealed. Those who were unfamiliar with this medium, popular in the United States in the 1980s, certainly experienced some trepidation while entrusting their carefully handcrafted project to the mercy of the heat beaming from the metal inside. They entered into the uncertain process with questions: Would the product of their labor melt? Would it be consumed or destroyed? Would the final product retain the unique colors of their choosing and maintain the distinct patterns of their discernment? The students helplessly glued their eyes to the window of the oven, watching—hearts leaping—as their art project twisted and turned in the heat. The project became a metaphor for their lives. The small plastic medallions endured the heat and toughened, sealed over time and in fire. The artworks became living symbols, both as souvenirs embodying the past and as expressions of life enfolding and becoming. Little did we know the very same symbol would serve as an emblem for our pilgrimage along the Ignatian Way, where the journey would be etched in their minds like the drawings on the medallions. What they were able to produce operated as a sacred symbol that captured the path where they had been as well as pointed toward the road where the spirit might be leading them. The physical mediated the sacred, and the sacred found a home in the physical.

Art along the Way

During a student pilgrimage, the art and cultural objects along the way become powerful places of encounter. Widening the aperture, it is fair to say that in most human contexts, the arts have an important role in both reflecting culture and also shaping it. Architecture, liturgical art, icons, statues, paintings, relics, and objects left by pilgrims (such as ex-votos) can all be important pedagogical tools to better understand the history of a site and the ritual practices that take place there.

To those who have engaged in the *Spiritual Exercises*, particularly Ignatian composition of place, it would come as no surprise that Ignatius focused on seemingly mundane details that he encouraged pilgrims to bring to the fore. For Ignatius, creation is saturated with the divine presence; nothing is profane. In fact, Ignatius was convinced that the divine "dwells" and "labors" in all things.[5] For that reason, in all things (*todas las cosas*), the person can encounter God. Ignatius's insistence on the sacredness of even so-called profane things underscores the value of the wide variety of encounters that occur on the road. Andrew Greeley, priest and sociologist, has written that the world of the Catholic is haunted by a sense that objects, events, and persons of daily life are revelations of grace and that "the artist (musician, storyteller, poet) is a 'sacrament maker,' a person who calls out of his materials insights and images into the meaning that lurks beneath them."[6] Art and physical objects bear the sacramental value that mediates and points toward transcendence.

---

5. Ignatius, *Personal Writings*, 230–37.
6. Andrew Greeley, *American Catholics since the Council: An Unauthorized Report* (Madison, WI: Thomas Moore, 1985), 222.

Objects are sites of encounter where the divine has found a home in the material world.

Art and objects also played pivotal roles in Ignatius's own pilgrimage experiences. One of these was the image of Our Lady of Montserrat, nestled high in the mountains of Spain, where Ignatius kept an all-night vigil during which he underwent a conversion of heart. After a long period of prayer, fasting, and reflection, he laid his sword below the image and, in doing so, professed a new life as a follower of Jesus. The image of the enthroned Black Madonna has been an important object of encounter for many pilgrims through the ages. Our Lady of Montserrat is attached to many legends and oral histories. Some say that the statue was carved by Saint Luke during biblical times and then carried to Spain by one of the apostles. During an invasion, the statue was said to have been hidden in a cave and was later discovered by shepherds who had been led to the hiding place upon following mysterious lights and heavenly song. A later bishop wanted to move the statue to Manresa, but it miraculously became heavier and heavier—Mary apparently wanted pilgrims to come to her on the mountain of Montserrat. The shrine has since been the site of many miracles and attracts over a million pilgrims a year.[7]

The image in this way engenders a sense of transtemporal *communitas*—of perceived connection across cultures and time. In addition to thinking about the community formed by those on pilgrimage, we mean to emphasize here the fact that an artwork or a built environment facilitates a tangible connection to all those who have come before and all those who will come again, not unlike

7. Michael P. Duricy, "Black Madonnas: Our Lady of Montserrat," on the website for the University of Dayton, March 26, 2008, https://udayton.edu/imri/mary/m/montserrat -black-madonna.php; and Sarah Jane Boss, *Empress and Handmaid: On Nature and Gender in the Cult of the Virgin Mary* (London: Bloomsbury, 2000), 5.

the invitation to join one's voice with the choir of saints and angels during a Roman Catholic eucharistic celebration.[8] It is a community formed across time and space, a connection to the pilgrims of the past and future, and a sense of closeness with the divine. One of the students shared a moment of letting go of unhelpful burdens keeping him from being a good priest and Christian: "The moment in which Ignatius placed his armor and sword before Our Lady of Montserrat . . . illustrates the power and beauty of conversion and turning one's life around."[9] The student went on to describe a significant vision in which Mary helped facilitate a leaving behind of burdens; together, they stamped out the unhelpful "negative messages that lead . . . to darkness and isolation."[10] The theme of reflecting on letting go of negativity appeared in many of the students' narratives post-Camino. Another shared, "As the scene unfolded, I wasn't before a statue of Mary. Instead, I was experiencing the real presence of Mary alive and well in my prayer. . . . I've found myself reflecting about what Ignatius had left behind, and I began to similarly ask myself if there is anything that I need to leave behind as I look ahead into the future."[11] The encounters at the shrine of the Madonna engendered a sense of the presence of the divine and a folding in of history experienced in real time.

Victor and Edith Turner posit pilgrimage as a liminoid phenomenon—that is, voluntary and nonroutine and distinct from

---

8. Victor Turner and Edith Turner, *Image and Pilgrimage in Christian Culture: Anthropological Perspectives* (New York: Columbia University Press, 2011), 13, 252–54. For more on this adaptation of the Turnerian notion of *communitas*, see Kathryn R. Barush, *Imaging Pilgrimage: Art as Embodied Experience* (New York: Bloomsbury, 2021).
9. A graduate student pilgrim reflecting on the experience of walking the Camino Ignaciano in June–July 2015.
10. A graduate student pilgrim reflecting on the experience of walking the Camino Ignaciano in June–July 2015.
11. A graduate student pilgrim reflecting on the experience of walking the Camino Ignaciano in June–July 2015.

A student pilgrim prays at the shrine of the Black Madonna of Montserrat along the Camino Ignaciano. Photo by Hung Pham, SJ.

a "liminal" experience that is usually understood as tied to a rite of passage within the structure of a set religious system or ritual.[12] They point to the transformative effect of approaching the final grotto or shrine, where sins are forgiven and the pilgrim identifies with "the symbolic representation of the founder's experiences"—hence "put[ting] on Christ Jesus as a paradigmatic mask."[13] This resonates with Ignatius's yearning to become more Christlike and with the student-pilgrims' framing of their pilgrimages as "walking in the footsteps of Ignatius"—an instrument of Christ—as a catalyst for their own ultimate growth and renewal. Ignatius symbolically (and literally) cast off his knightly attire and sword and clothed himself as a pilgrim in sackcloth with a gourd to drink from. When he arrived at Montserrat, he kept vigil all night and decided to "clothe himself in the armour of Christ."[14] While at Montserrat, Ignatius made a written confession for three days, which is compatible with the Turners' notion of the transformative effect of reconciliation during this phase of pilgrimage.

Before we visited the mountain, we had already encountered the Madonna of Montserrat. In fact, even before we left our classroom in Berkeley, we had read of Ignatius's deep Marian devotion and his vigil in front of the image. Then along the pilgrimage route from Loyola to Montserrat, we saw several reproductions of the statue. Some of them were placed quite high up and behind tall wrought-iron gates. A couple of these had long ribbons like a necklace around the Madonna, attached to laminated prayer cards that hung through the bars of the gates. Although I have not been

---

12. As Deborah Ross has stated, "As modern pilgrimage in complex postindustrial societies is voluntary, [the Turners] described it as a 'liminoid' experience, rather than a liminal one in the rite-of-passage sense." Deborah Ross, introduction to Turner and Turner, *Image and Pilgrimage*, xxxi.

13. Turner and Turner, *Image and Pilgrimage*, 11.

14. Ignatius, *Personal Writings*, 17.

able to confirm this with certainty, I imagine that these are in the vein of contact relics, which are bits of card, textiles (such as ribbons), or religious medals that are, in an act of piety, touched to a sacred image or relic. In her comprehensive essay on the origin of third-class relics and modern and medieval understandings of their use, Julia M. H. Smith has noted that the classification is "a mid-twentieth-century variant on the categories prescribed in post-Tridentine canon law" and highlights a key point, which is the "tension between spontaneous and officialized veneration."[15] A connection can be drawn between medieval and modern sensibilities; in the distant past, and still today (as shown through this research), relics are objects that "derive their meaning from the subjective understanding of those who . . . cherished them."[16] These objects are often carried as pilgrimage souvenirs. As Jane Garnett and Gervase Rosser posit in their book on the "enduring Western belief" in the supernatural power of images in the northwest of Italy and beyond, "There is clearly a reciprocal relationship between copy and prototype, of which the history of image cults can show many examples."[17] The laminated images of the Madonna hanging from a reproduction of the image are exciting previews of what the pilgrim will encounter at Montserrat.

It is easy to see how representations of a holy person can serve as a way to bring history to life. We have already discussed the pious legends attached to the making of the image and how it helped

---

15. Julia M. H. Smith, "Relics: An Evolving Tradition in Latin Christianity," in *Saints and Sacred Matter: The Cult of Relics in Byzantium and Beyond*, ed. Cynthia Hahn and Holger Klein (Washington, DC: Dumbarton Oaks, 2015), 42.

16. Smith, 60. See also p. 53: "Medieval discourses about relics were the product of the educated, clerical, and monastic elite. Participation in the cult of relics was far more widespread, however, and we can establish what a large circle of people regarded as relics by interrogating the evidence of what they collected and treasured."

17. Jane Garnett and Gervase Rosser, *Spectacular Miracles: Transforming Images in Italy from the Renaissance to the Present* (London: Reaktion, 2013), 195.

focus Saint Ignatius of Loyola's prayers to the Virgin Mary and to God as he felt their presence during his vigil—an experience shared by the students. Many of the students mentioned Ignatius's moment of leaving behind the sword as framing their own experiences at Montserrat. They described a sense of renewal and change going forward, similar to a renewal of baptismal vows in a liturgical context, both on the pilgrimage and in their lives. This is consistent with the Turners' theory that these "symbol vehicles" spur *communitas* and engender a sense of rebirth and spiritual renewal.[18] In this instance, the Virgin Mary, as Mother of God and a vessel of the incarnation, became another place of encounter during the pilgrimage. The representation of Mary and Christ in the form of a statue in and of itself reminds us of the importance of matter; after all, Jesus himself took on a material body when he became human.[19] These representations, as Ignatius learned, are sacramental as well

---

18. The Turners argue that

   the outward form of a symbol is connected more closely with its orectic (or emotional/volitional) pole of significance than with its normative (or ideological) pole. Association and analogy connect the sensorily perceived symbol-vehicle, or image, to referents of a dominantly emotional or wishful character. . . . New significance may then be generated as devotees associate the particularized, personalized image with their own hopes and sorrows as members of a particular community with a specific history. . . . The original signified is not completely replaced, but rather fused with and partially altered by the new signified; or it may coexist with the new as part of a mosaic of meaning. . . . It is not idolatrous worship of the signifier at the expense of the signified, that is here in question—as theological polemic has too often asserted. (Turner and Turner, *Image and Pilgrimage*, 143–44)

19. As John of Damascus wrote, and as several modern papal documents have emphasized in relation to the art of the Catholic Church, "Either we must suppress the sacred nature of all these things, or we must concede to the tradition of the Church the veneration of the images of God and that of the friends of God who are sanctified by the name they bear, and for this reason are possessed by the grace of the Holy Spirit. Do not, therefore, offend matter: it is not contemptible, because nothing that God has made is contemptible." *Contra imaginum calumniatores orationes tres*, 1, 16, ed. Bonifatius Kotter, 89–90, as cited by Benedict XVI, "John Damascene," General Audience, Vatican, May 6, 2009, https://w2.vatican.va/content/benedict-xvi/en/audiences/2009/documents/hf_ben-xvi_aud_20090506.html.

as important components of the composition of place and certainly took on this role for the student pilgrims.

Another Marian site that we encountered was the sanctuary of La Virgen María de Aránzazu (Basque for "thorn," or in Castilian, *espinar*). To Íñigo, Aránzazu embodied a step in both familiar and unknown directions. Like other members of the Loyola family who had come to pray there, Íñigo had knelt down, his eyes fixed on the smiling Virgin with baby Jesus on her lap. It was there where he sought the grace of confirmation in his discernment to move forward on his pilgrimage.[20] The modern architecture of the Basilica at Aránzazu is arresting. It was built in the 1950s by architects Francisco Javier Sáenz de Oiza and Luis Laorga, with many other artisans who contributed to the art in the interior of the space. Upon entering the church, our group was scattered in all different directions, mesmerized by the statues, stained glass windows, and paintings. The quiet tranquility and dimly lit candles drew us to the front of the sanctuary, where we encountered an image of the Virgin sitting on a thornbush, presiding over the sacred space—one hand holding the globe, the other her baby. There was a rather big and rusty cowbell at her feet, which captured our curiosity. It is attached to the story of a shepherd who heard and followed the sound of a bell, which drew him to the mysterious carving of the Virgin, hidden in a thornbush.

The sacred objects within bring to mind the journey of Ignatius and, by proxy, engender the inherent link to the *civitas Dei* toward which all Christians proceed as "strangers and pilgrims." As Pham recalled later in an essay we published on our experiences there, "The space was a stunning, airy, modern interior that showcased the ancient objects that informed our experience there. The serene

---

20. Ricardo García-Villoslada, *San Ignacio de Loyola: Nueva Biografía* (Madrid: Biblioteca de Autores Cristianos, 1987), 185.

beauty of the sanctuary slowly unarmed the different preoccupations of our various attachments, physically or mentally, and drew the pilgrims ever closer to its solemn sanctum. It was not we who found the road, but the road and its subtle yet prevailing beauty that found us."[21]

The experience reflects but also crucially continues what Ignatius had encountered at Loyola, Aránzazu, the sacred mountain of Montserrat, and the cave at Manresa. As we have seen, art and space encountered in the context of a student pilgrimage can be transformative in many ways. The case study presented here has focused on the Ignatian Camino, where it has brought history to life in a culturally contextualized way. It offered crucial insights into the study of historic and contemporary lived religion, devotional practice, and popular piety. For our students who were on Camino as part of a class on Ignatian spirituality, these Marian images also impacted their spiritual formation and health and well-being. In other settings—for example, a pilgrimage focused on social justice—art can become a powerful tool toward shaping change and raising critical consciousness. At somewhere like the GTU, which represents so many of the world's religions, art can become a nexus for dialogical encounter.

Art as a Souvenir

In the Middle Ages as today, objects brought back from a sacred journey can serve as a way to reenact an experience of sacred travel, as a mnemonic device, and as a talking point to prompt sharing about the pilgrim's experience. These items can be used as a pedagogical

---

21. Hung Pham, SJ, in Hung Pham and Kathryn Barush, "From Swords to Shoes: Encountering Grace on the Camino Ignaciano," *Practical Matters*, June 28, 2016, http://practicalmattersjournal.org/?p=2889.

tool to show, rather than tell, students how the material and visual culture of religion can provide a lens through which to explore a number of themes and ideas. For example, I have a scallop shell that I brought back from the Camino de Santiago that I often pass around class as an introduction to the material culture of pilgrimage. The students usually make formal observations at first: they point out the materiality (it is a natural shell on which is painted a red swordlike insignia; it has two holes through which is passed a red cord). Then we deepen our thinking in order to postulate what this object might be used for and what Christian iconography it relates to. For example, could it have been used by early pilgrims as a begging bowl or water vessel? It has a cord through it—could it have been worn by pilgrims to indicate that they had traveled to the shrine of Saint James? With some research, legends, oral histories, and hagiographic accounts are uncovered; for example, there is an account that when the body of the apostle Saint James washed up on shore in Galicia, he was covered in scallops. I usually point out that scallop-shaped vessels are used in baptism, which often leads to a fruitful discussion of the possibility of renewal while on pilgrimage. Another student pointed out that for her, the ridges on the scallop shell are symbolic of all roads leading to Santiago de Compostela.

Souvenirs can also provide important insights into devotional practices that pilgrims participate in both today and through history. For example, the Catholic popular devotional practice of pressing a prayer card or ribbon to the reliquaries protecting the remains of the saint or even (as Bede tells us) gathering the dust that accrued on the sacred container to make what is popularly called a "contact" (or "third-class") relic has a long history.[22] The practice has roots in

22. See, for example, Bede, *Hist. Eccl.*, lib. iv, C. iii: "Sometimes [tombs of the saints] arose as tiny Minster-like buildings, overshadowing the silver or the stone case which held

the ancient world and was encouraged in Patristic writing; Gregory, Eusebius, and Augustine all discuss third-class relics in the form of filings from Saint Peter's chains, oil, and flowers from the holy land, respectively. There is also surviving extratextual evidence of these practices, including an arresting sixth-century reliquary box from Palestine or Syria (now in the Vatican's Museo Sacro).[23] It has a cover decorated with tempera and gold leaf on wood depicting scenes from the life of Christ. Inside are stones and bits of dirt from the Holy Land, each relating to the story that took place at the sites where they were collected.

Another example of objects that enact an experience of sacred travel might be the practice of sewing pilgrimage souvenirs in the form of thin lead badges into illuminated manuscripts, which Megan Foster-Campbell has described as an "aid for personal devotion beyond the temporal and physical experience of a pilgrimage journey—facilitated mental or virtual pilgrimage for the book owner, through memory or imagination."[24] Then as in now, displaying, looking at, holding, or even telling a friend about a pilgrimage souvenir can engender a reenactment or remembrance of a pilgrimage. As we entered the Church of the Gesù in Rome, some of the students quietly took out their plastic medallions that we

the saints' relics, and allowing, through a hole or window in the side, those who might like, to stretch forth their hands and gather the dust which lay upon the coffin lid." In Daniel Rock, *The Church of Our Fathers, as Seen in St. Osmund's Rite for the Cathedral of Salisbury* (London, 1852), 353–54 and note 19. For a discussion of medieval contact relics, see also Robert Bartlett, *Why Can the Dead Do Such Great Things? Saints and Worshippers from the Martyrs to the Reformation* (Princeton, NJ: Princeton University Press, 2013).

23. The box was recently displayed in the exhibition *Treasures of Heaven: Saints, Relics, and Devotion in Medieval Europe* at the Cleveland Museum of Art, the Walters Art Museum, and the British Museum. Martina Bagnoli et al., *Treasures of Heaven* (London: British Museum Press, 2010), catalog 37, fig. 13.

24. Megan Foster-Campbell, "Pilgrims' Badges in Late Medieval Devotional Manuscripts," in *Push Me, Pull You: Imaginative and Emotional Interaction in Late Medieval and Renaissance Art*, vol. 1, ed. S. Blick and L. D. Gelfand (Leiden, Netherlands: Brill, 2011), 229.

made in class, described above, and gently pressed them against the altar. Some blessed their artworks with the holy water. As their life journey continued, so did their icons, continuing to take shape, a living memory.

Journaling, drawing, and photography are also ways for student pilgrims to mediate and capture their experiences on the road, and such objects can serve a similar purpose. While some students prefer written reflections, others might appreciate the immediacy of taking a photograph of a moment along the way or creating a sketch of a landscape. Again, there is a continuity with a historical practice in terms of one pilgrim's record engendering an embodied experience for another. Recent scholarship in the field of medieval studies has established the importance of manuscripts, maps, and labyrinths as sites of mental or stationary pilgrimage for those who could not travel for a variety of reasons.[25] One such example is the story of the Dominican friar Felix Fabri, who was known for recording his own pilgrimages in various formats, some geared toward the laity and some for his brothers. Fabri was approached in the 1490s by a group of cloistered nuns who desired a devotional exercise so that they, too, could receive the spiritual benefits of pilgrimage without having to break their promise of a life that was sheltered from the outside world.[26] Fabri produced *Die Sionpilger*, a pilgrimage by proxy in the form of a day-to-day guidebook to Santiago de Compostela, Jerusalem, and Rome. Fabri's guidebook sent the pilgrim on an imaginative journey of a thousand miles without having to take a single step.

25. See, for example, Daniel K. Connolly, "Imagined Pilgrimages in Gothic Art: Maps, Manuscripts, and Labyrinths" (PhD diss., University of Chicago, 1998), 1; and Kathryn M. Rudy, "A Guide to Mental Pilgrimage: Paris, Bibliotheque de L'Arsenal Ms. 212," *Zeitschrift für Kunstgeschichte* 63 Bd., H. 4 (2000): 494–515.
26. Kathryne Beebe, "Reading Mental Pilgrimage in Context: The Imaginary Pilgrims and Real Travels of Felix Fabri's 'Die Sionpilger,'" *Essays in Medieval Studies* 25 (2008): 39–70.

This chapter emerged out of the Covid-19 pandemic, when many pilgrimages have been canceled or curtailed, and this idea of pilgrimage records, souvenirs, and narratives spurring an embodied experience for others has taken on a renewed significance. The idea of transferring the sacredness from one landscape to another has become a way to respond to Covid-19 as well as to what has been called the "twin pandemic" of racial injustice. Sara Postlethwaite, a sister of the Verbum Dei Missionary Fraternity and student in Barush's Virtual Sacred Spaces course, decided to create her own route as a space for reflection, mourning, and prayer. Postlethwaite mapped Saint Kevin's Way, a nineteen-mile pilgrimage route in County Wicklow, Ireland onto a series of daily 1.5-mile circuits in the urban environs of Daly City, California. The Wicklow Way rambles along roads and countryside from Hollywood to the ruins of the monastery that Saint Kevin, a sixth-century abbot, had founded in Glendalough. Postlethwaite had intended to travel back to her native Ireland in the spring of 2020 to walk the route in person, but due to pandemic-related travel restrictions, she brought the pilgrimage to her home in Daly City. Every so often, Postlethwaite would check in on Google Maps to see where she was along the Irish route, pivoting the camera to see surrounding trees or, at one point, finding herself in the center of an old stone circle. After each day's walk, Postlethwaite paused at the shed at her community house, where she had drawn a to-scale version of the Market Cross at Glendalough. As she traced the intersecting Celtic knots, circles, and the image of the crucified Christ with her chalk, she reflected not just on the suffering caused by the pandemic but also on issues of racism, justice, and privilege. In particular, she remembered Ahmaud Arbery, a Black jogger shot by two white men in a fatal confrontation in February 2020. She inscribed his name on the chalk cross. Several joined Postlethwaite's walk in solidarity, both in the United

States and overseas. While projects like this may not solve the many issues of social injustice plaguing our world, they can bring people together in solidarity as a step toward healing.

While remaining in self-isolation in Saint Louis, Pham directed an online pilgrimage following Ignatius's footsteps virtually hosted by Saint Ignatius Church in Singapore that gathered more than four hundred pilgrims from England, the Philippines, Malaysia, Singapore, the United States, and Vietnam. Every day, after having meditated on each Ignatian landmark, each pilgrim was committed to walk in their own cities. As a result, Loyola, Montserrat, Manresa, and so on became alive in cities across Southeast Asia and North America. More importantly, while the world was forced into isolation, the breakout room and the chat function on Zoom became sacred places of encounter where pilgrims continued to form the *communitas* and the *communitas* continued to nourish them.

While we were drafting this essay, one of our student pilgrims came across a photo of our group on the Camino Ignaciano website and posted it on social media. The Camino Foundation is currently seeking support toward a potential reopening of the route to coincide with the "Ignatian Year" anniversary in 2022, if this proves safe. The student found a photo of our 2014 Camino group on the landing page of the website with the banner "2022 has already started." We have been living with photos of the journey for so long that I really did not expect to experience a moment of temporal dislocation when I saw the image. It was one I had never seen before, and it was particularly moving, especially after having lived under stay-at-home orders for a full year. The image shows us arriving at Manresa—smiling, arms in the air. Two of our students, Michael from Kenya and Sr. Daniella from Vietnam, are wearing their souvenir T-shirts that we were given upon arrival in Manresa with a graphic showing a stylized map of the route. Another student, Ana, had posted a screenshot of the image with the words, "Still savoring the *gracia*. Much love!"

With her electronic postcard, we were transported back to that moment. Whoever clicked the link would learn a little about Ignatius and the pilgrimage route based on his own journey—but as we have shown, with plenty of room for personal experiences and learning.

Conclusion

The ancient pathways that our Camino students traveled served as roads not only to and from sites and shrines but inward. History blossomed in living color all around us pilgrims, students and teachers, in Spanish polychrome altarpieces from Ignatius's time to the ancient trees along the route we traversed. As we walked, the ancient pathways transcended time and space as they mapped onto our own experiences and stories. To conclude with the words of one of the student pilgrims, "That outward journey was a symbol of what continues to take place in my soul."[27] This essay has sought to triangulate the interconnectedness between art as an object of pilgrimage, as a record of pilgrimage, and as a pilgrimage in and of itself. Just like the interlinking of the senses of the term *pilgrimage* as a journey on foot and a journey through life, art can both reflect and engender an experience of sacred journey. Sometimes, art praxis can become an embodied experience for the creator, viewer, or both. Although the primary focus was on the art encountered before, during, and after a student journey along the Camino Ignaciano, the pedagogical approaches described can apply to any religious pilgrimage along which sacred art and objects are encountered.

---

27. A graduate student pilgrim reflecting on the experience of walking the Camino Ignaciano in June–July 2015.

Questions for Reflection

1. As you reminisce on various objects located in your home or housing, what memories does each of them stir up for you?
2. If you were to chain these memories together, what inner movements might you detect? What patterns do you see emerging? What have you learned about yourself? About others? And about transcendence—something beyond yourselves at work?
3. If you were to capture these movements and patterns in a sketch, an image, a song, a piece of jewelry, a quilt, a poem, or a drawing to be shared with a friend, what might it look like?

Select Annotated Bibliography

Barush, Kathryn. *Imaging Pilgrimage: Art as Embodied Experience.* New York: Bloomsbury, 2021.

A first-of-its-kind exploration of art and music created during or after a pilgrimage in order to engender the experience for others. Barush brings various fields into conversation by offering a number of lenses and theoretical approaches (materialist, kinesthetic, haptic, synesthetic) that engage objects as radical sites of encounter, activated through religious and ritual praxis and negotiated with not just the eyes but a multiplicity of senses.

Coleman, Simon, and John Elsner. *Pilgrimage: Past and Present in the World Religions.* Cambridge, MA: Harvard University Press, 1995.

John Elsner, an art historian as well as a classicist, and
Simon Coleman, an anthropologist, bring an interdisciplinary
and interreligious perspective to the study of pilgrimage.
This is a good introductory text that explores the origins
and theology of pilgrimage across religious traditions. Each
chapter ends with a look at the visual and material culture of
pilgrimage as well as the importance of art along the way and
as a souvenir of the sacred journey.

Marsh, Robert. "Id Quod Vola: The Erotic Grace of the Second
Week." *The Way* 45, no. 4 (October 2006): 7–19.

An excellent guide to Ignatian contemplation providing
great insight into how Ignatius maps the dynamic of the
Second Week of the *Spiritual Exercises* after his inability to
stay in Jerusalem and the early companions' failed attempt to
make a pilgrimage to the Holy Land.

McManamon, John, SJ. *The Text and Contexts of Ignatius Loyola's
"Autobiography."* New York: Fordham University Press, 2013.

One of the latest in-depth studies on Ignatius of Loyola's
Autobiography revealing the rich meanings of the various
biblical themes and spiritual symbols embedded in how
Ignatius's life story was told and composed.

Standaert, Nicolas. "The Composition of Place: Creating Space of
an Encounter." *The Way* 46, no. 1 (January 2007): 7–20.

A deep intuition on the various spiritual movements that
have been instilled in the Ignatian practice of "composition
of place," in turn inspiring and empowering others to remain
creative in structuring a space of encounter with the divine in
their spiritual practices.

Chapter 5

Pilgrimage as Comedy

(Re)Forming Individuals into Community

Eileen C. Sweeney
Boston College

The struggle and the gift of pilgrimage is that it is not only the "journey of life" in microcosm but also society in microcosm.[1] Whether or not it is an explicit subject of a pilgrimage class, one of its most important tasks is the creation of a community from its disparate individuals. I did not realize before I led a pilgrimage of students on a two-hundred-mile trek on the Camino in Spain that I would have to be so fully intentional about fostering community among those joining together for a pilgrimage journey. What I explore here are the difficulties and rewards of forming an authentic community along with the questions, sources, and activities that helped us on this path. I do so using the notion of pilgrimage as comedy along with the social theories of Jean-Jacques Rousseau and Hannah Arendt.

---

1. I am grateful to my colleagues Jeffrey Bloechl and Holly Vandewall. Jeff designed the Camino Pilgrimage class and I (literally and figuratively) followed in his footsteps; Holly led the Camino class the year before I did and imparted a great deal of wisdom about student/faculty dynamics as well as suggested readings, many of which are in my annotated bibliography. I would not have been able to lead the class without the help of both of them.

Of the many applicants for the ten places in the pilgrimage course, I chose a very diverse group, not just in race, ethnicity, and gender, but also in sexual orientation, social class, and immigration stories. I had freshman to seniors, theology and economics majors, natural science and business majors, and philosophy and political science majors. Some were more activist, others more contemplative; some were religiously committed and observant, others searching for or on hold with religious practice; some were from multireligious family backgrounds—from one woman with Hindu, Jewish, and Christian family members to the daughter of Christian evangelical missionaries in China—and many things in between.

Such a group would not cohere by itself. Moreover, I was asking for a much higher degree of connection and community than I would seek to create in an ordinary college class. Though we had a shared desire to make the pilgrimage and to discern and reflect on our ultimate values and identities, the crew I assembled brought to mind the collection of pilgrims in Chaucer's *Canterbury Tales* and made me see the narrative form of our journey as comedy, and at least equal measures high and low comedy. Chaucer sets up his tales with an offer made by the host that all the participants will tell stories, and the one whose story is judged to be the best will be treated to a meal by all the others. Like Chaucer's pilgrims, my students had a mixed set of incentives. They were taking the class for a grade and so had to perform as the class required for a reward external to the pilgrimage itself. In one sense, of course, the external motivators, the credits and the grade, were designed to support and reinforce the internal personal motives. In another sense, however, the class (whose title captures the internal personal goal: "Self-knowledge and Discernment") tempted the students to "perform" authenticity, a contradiction in terms, and set me up as the host and "judge" of their tales, which, unlike Chaucer's pilgrims',

are their own. Another layer of complication is the expectation of a highly meaningful experience on the pilgrimage. This threatens to create a break between the self who is living the experience and the self who is waiting for and observing the meaningful experience. Like taking photos on vacation, pilgrims are in danger of standing outside of their journey, performing and presenting it in photos.

Pilgrimage per se has the structure of romance or quest. The heroic, physical tasks are walking and contending with weather, blisters, sore knees, hunger, and thirst. There is an *agon* or struggle, a "sequence of marvelous adventures" on the way to the completion of the quest.[2] As the literary critic Northrop Frye notes, "The quest-romance is the search of the libido or desiring self for a fulfilment that will deliver it from the anxieties of reality but still contain that reality."[3] The students, who signed up for a class on self-knowledge, who wanted to walk two hundred miles across Spain, were both on a search for deliverance from anxieties, to find a more authentic self with which they could return to their lives, and looking for a challenging adventure.

However, within that larger arc of quest-romance, there is comedy. The quest's task is the completion of the pilgrimage, but the comedic task is the refounding and reconstruction of a flawed society. Society must change in order to incorporate the new or marginalized members, by either transforming or even ejecting those who are unreasonably preventing social integration. Frye, my guide to narrative forms, describes one typical form of comedy as "the drama of the green world" (think *A Midsummer Night's Dream*) in which all escape a corrupt society to a "green world" outside its bounds, ultimately to return to and reform/refound society.[4] The pilgrimage follows this narrative first by escaping the habits, arbitrary rules, and laws of society to go on pilgrimage, not forever, but in order to find out what to keep and what to reject when one returns. In classical comedy, all the characters must be integrated into a new community with no one voluntarily or involuntarily excluded. This comedic resolution is the only means to completing the quest of the pilgrimage, for only in authentic friendships can the pilgrims successfully discern their true selves and future paths. Like comedy, our beginning stage was conflict, followed by disorder and

---

2. Northrop Frye, *Anatomy of Criticism: Four Essays* (Princeton, NJ: Princeton University Press, 1973), 192.
3. Frye, 193.
4. Frye, 182.

reshuffling, to struggling toward resolution, to returning to ordinary life transformed.

One of my favorite short passages for meditation and for thinking about pilgrimage is from the twelfth-century canon and theologian Hugh of Saint Victor: "The person who finds his homeland sweet is still a tender beginner; he to whom every soil is his native one is already strong; but he is perfect to whom the whole world is a place of exile."[5] These are the stages of learning and, of course, life. They are also a way of thinking about the stages of the pilgrimage as comedy.

Act 1: The Tender Beginner

The image that comes to mind as our group began to meet for our biweekly seminar was of people trying to get comfortable in their chairs, looking around a bit warily. I felt like Chaucer's host as I surveyed the personalities assembled. Some seemed even to fit in Chaucer's roles—we had our knight (both male and female, with noble motives and graciousness to all), our squire (courtly at all times, making sure we all had adequate wine and food), our parson (who became everyone's favored companion and confidante) and prioress (both delicate and gentle), as well as a socially agreeable friar, even our wife of Bath (the advisor on matters of the heart), and our clerk (hungry for knowledge and experiences). We did not have Chaucer's corrupt characters, but we had one or two who were less mature and one or two who drifted in and out of being seriously engaged with the project of pilgrimage as a spiritual and psychological task. Both the pleasure in each other's company and the

---

5. Hugh of St. Victor, *Didascalicon of Hugh of St. Victor: A Medieval Guide to the Arts*, trans. J. Taylor (New York: Columbia University Press, 1991), bk. 3, chap. 19, p. 101. I have adjusted Taylor's translation of "exilium" as "foreign land."

tensions only increased on the trip as we walked and ate and rested together and as we slept in dormitory settings with group showers. Such conditions had a way of exposing our foibles and weaknesses, stripping away the carefully curated self and studied performance to which we would normally retreat.

Comedy's two emotions, according to Frye, corresponding to the pity and fear central to the catharsis of tragedy, are sympathy and ridicule.[6] Rightly so, because a community is created by sympathy and fissured by ridicule. Frye thus helped me understand that the attitude most to be feared was sarcasm, a form of ridicule and ironic distance. This posed the greatest danger to the trip, since the whole point was to be authentic and vulnerable, not to stand outside the trip as an observer. I feared that my disparate group would make connections but in the form of cliques who would "share" gossip and inside jokes, making the whole group the opposite of the safe and authentic community I sought to form and making comedic integration and resolution impossible.

Rousseau's *Reveries of a Solitary Walker* became a cautionary tale about how our "green world" community might fail. Rousseau writes the *Reveries* in a retreat from the dystopic social world in which he lived. While Rousseau's *Confessions* reveals his personal inability to accept or be accepted by any of the societies he attempted to found or join and the *Reveries* recounts his final retreat from any further attempts to do so, his *Discourse on the Origin of Inequality* reveals why society fails to become a community, a reason grounded not in nature but in society: the corrosive effects of self-esteem. As opposed to natural self-love, which seeks one's self-preservation, self-esteem is the desire to be desired, to be *seen* as better than others. This is not the brutal desire to dominate or to amass wealth or power but,

---

6. Frye, *Anatomy of Criticism*, 177.

rather, the *cause* of those desires and, hence, the cause of inequality. In the grips of self-esteem, we rewrite Aristotle's maxim about the necessity of friendship: no one would choose to have every good or power greater than others on the condition of not being *known and seen by others* to have them. The need to be desired is the need to be *seen as more desirable* than the next person, to win the competition. The desire to have more stuff (food, land, clothes, cars, etc.) is neither primary nor natural for Rousseau; natural desire is only for what is required for physical survival. The rest is to wear as a badge to make us stand out for and, hence, against others.

Rousseau places the origins of competition and conflict in our vulnerability to each other, painting a picture not of the strong trying to outdo one another but of each and every one caught in the look of the other, in those early social gatherings around the campfire: "Each one began to look at the others and to want to be looked at himself, and public esteem had a value."[7] This vulnerable moment of wanting to be desired is so intolerable, it is no wonder that we attempt in one way or another to escape our vulnerability to the other. For Rousseau, we try to secure our desirability by differentiating ourselves from others, becoming better looking, better spoken, better equipped with material things: "From these first preferences were born vanity and contempt on the one hand, and shame and envy on the other."[8] The drive to distinguish oneself from others, to exaggerate and cultivate differences, to convert every difference into a hierarchy is the secret sauce of social life, transforming it into the zero-sum game we all know, the dystopia it feels impossible to escape. For Rousseau, self-esteem deprives us of

---

7. Jean-Jacques Rousseau, *Discourse on the Origin and Foundations of Inequality among Men in the Basic Political Writings*, trans. Donald A. Cress (Indianapolis: Hackett, 1987), 64.
8. Rousseau, 64.

our very selfhood, making us live only in the eyes and opinions of others rather than in ourselves. To be without regard from others is to slip into a kind of nonexistence.

On the Camino, we strip away many of the tools we use to create social hierarchy and come much closer to Rousseau's state of nature. With the limitation of our needs and, hence, desires—food, drink, rest, company—and our shared (and only) task of walking about fifteen miles per day, the playing field had been greatly leveled. We had minimal belongings—only two changes of radically utilitarian clothes, no room for doing one's hair or makeup, no way to cover up what one looks like walking all day in the heat or rain, dust or mud.

But alas, we found, we were not in the state of nature but in the campfire gathering where society forms. Quickly, new hierarchies of difference began to emerge: who could walk faster and longer, who could walk without injury and without blisters, who had or needed walking sticks. We had not so much escaped the vagaries of society but had created a more intense version of it, partly because our usual tools for our social defense, those that help us cement our position in the social hierarchy (wealth and social status), had been stripped away by the conditions of pilgrimage.

In the first half of Rousseau's discourse, where there is no inequality (and also no social life), nature is homogeneous, and its gifts are abundant and easy to acquire. But in the second half, part of what both generates the need for social connection and also simultaneously creates the conditions for self-esteem is the growing heterogeneity of nature—hills and valleys, heat and cold, water and drought. The Camino, while not over dramatically difficult terrain, still has a variable landscape, climbing and descending, with weather conditions that range between too hot and too cold, too wet and too dry for perfectly comfortable hiking. It is not easy. So we had to rely on one another—an injured walker needed help climbing or descending, needed the loan of a walking stick or someone else to carry some of their heavier items, and slower walkers needed companions. A subtle but real struggle occurred three times per day (late morning, lunch, and late afternoon). The rule was that people could walk as they wished at their own pace, alone or with others, but the first to arrive at a designated rest stop three times a day had to wait for the last person to arrive at the stop before taking off on the next segment of the day's walk. Some were too antsy to wait for others to catch up, and others simply wanted to be first, vying to be the fastest, while those who rolled in last were dismayed to watch the first arrivals leave as soon as they showed up. In the first couple of days, a group of students I fell into step with confessed that the discussion of the day was about which member of the group would win in *The Hunger Games* (they all agreed that it would be an especially competent, tall, strong, and brilliant woman in the group). Hardly a world without rankings!

Something similar keeps happening to Rousseau in the *Reveries*—every time he seems to create a new and authentic relationship, something makes things slide back into the kinds of demands and competitions that derive from the need for self-esteem, that recognition from the other that drives us to try for the unwinnable goal of having others prefer us even to themselves. In the moments where Rousseau finds peace, it is because he finds a way to approximate vegetative existence, eschewing social life altogether.[9] There is no comic resolution, no anagnorisis about self or other that will allow the refounding of a nontoxic society. Comic anagnorisis is the recognition of one's true self that makes the marriage (or other social bonds) possible; hence, the curtain can close

---

9. Jean-Jacques Rousseau, *The Reveries of a Solitary Walker*, trans. Charles E. Butterworth (Indianapolis, IN: Hackett, 1992). See, for example, walks 5, 6, and 8 (pp. 62–88, 110–20).

on the comedic "happily ever after." But for Rousseau, recognition can never be mutual; it is always a toxic zero-sum game.

Thus though we had stripped away many of the layers of our social identity, making us both more open and more vulnerable to new social arrangements, this alone would not create a good society. Just as in any comedy, before the resolution, there is a good deal of mischief, many misunderstandings and false starts in "the green world" exactly because it is lacking the usual constraints of normal (even if badly) ordered life. We had our own mixed-up society (think of the mayhem of the middle acts of *A Midsummer Night's Dream*). The task, then, was to take these "tender beginners" quite literally beyond their comfort zones in this "green world" toward personal and social integration rather than its opposite.

Act 2: Every Soil Is Native

While Rousseau articulates the *problem* of society, Hannah Arendt articulates a more compelling solution, in my view, than Rousseau ever devised. For Arendt, the peculiar human condition is one of "plurality," which is different from both "individuality" and uniformity. We are "plural," she writes, "because we are all the same, that is, human, in such a way that nobody is ever the same as anyone else who ever lived, lives, or will live."[10] Every birth is the appearance of someone with new possibilities, new responses, new inventions.[11] For Arendt, being both equal to and unique among others makes speech/disclosure both possible and necessary. Because we are all human, and thus equal, we *can* understand each other, and because we are distinct, we all have something, that very uniqueness, to reveal.[12]

---

10. Hannah Arendt, *The Human Condition* (Garden City, NY: Doubleday Anchor, 1959), 8.
11. Arendt, 9.
12. Arendt, 175–76.

Arendt elevates the desire to reveal and be recognized as a unique individual into a basic human desire. It's not something extra but the substance of what it is to be human. To engage in that process of revelation and recognition with those we usually don't is part of the substance and not a mere accidental by-product of pilgrimage.

We are all characterizable in general terms applicable to whole groups, and that includes not only the features that are the subject of political debate (race, gender, sexual orientation, ethnicity, class, ability/disability) but all the characteristics that confer or degrade status, everything that can be compared and ranked (appearance, intelligence, education, income, wealth). In the microcosm of my Camino class, all these differences were represented. If these features of ourselves were all we wanted recognition for, Arendt's social world would be defined by the same kind of competition and ever-increasing inequality described by Rousseau. Arendt, however, proposes a distinction between these kinds of features, which outline *what* we are, and those that reveal *who* we are as individuals, not a list of our accomplishments or social categories but our actions and stories. The political movements for recognition of races other than white, for women as opposed to men, of LGBTQIA identities as opposed to cisgender/heterosexual identity might seem to contradict this notion, since these movements seem to aim at the recognition of "what" rather than "who." But to be in a dominant group is to have one's full humanity recognized; the ultimate privilege of the dominant caste is to be a "who" and not just a "what." To recognize a marginalized group's status is to make it possible for the individuals within it to be and be seen as "whos," not just as members of a lesser group, either demeaned or not seen at all.

We all recognize what it is to be summed up and thus dismissed as *only* this, that, or the other thing. Not to be seen as worthy of recognition as an individual is *the* moment in the primal high school scene. We have all lived through this, all seen the movie variations on the "nerd" asking the "cheerleader" to go out only to be jeered at by the object of their interest as essentially not existing as a possible partner in a relationship, because they are not recognizable as an individual. And we have all seen the resolution in the recognition (the comic anagnorisis) of the character's full humanity and uniqueness, revealing that they are a "who" and not just a "what." The aspiration of romantic love, with all its unrealistic and contradictory wishes, has as perhaps first among its desires the recognition of one's uniqueness. No one wants to be loved for their "what-ness" but for their "who-ness." Hence its location as the scene of unpredictability and injury as well as deep longing.

Becoming "who" we are only takes place among others for Arendt. For, as she writes, "without a space of appearance and without trusting in action and speech as a mode of being together, neither the reality of one's self, of one's own identity, nor the reality of the surrounding world can be established beyond doubt."[13] She characterizes this space of appearance as the realm of "togetherness," a world of being "with" rather than a world divided into those who are for and against us.[14] Engaging with the "who," what she calls "action," is unpredictable and uncontrollable because we reveal ourselves and leave others free to respond. But as Arendt writes, "The impossibility of remaining unique masters of what [we] do, of knowing its consequences and relying upon the future, is the price [we] pay for plurality and reality, for the joy of inhabiting together with others a world whose reality is guaranteed for each by the presence of all."[15]

---

13. Arendt, 208.
14. Arendt, 180.
15. Arendt, 244.

Arendt's account shows how and why the projects of self-knowledge and connection with the other are linked. Our inauthenticity, our way of constructing a sense of self by "what" rather than "who" we are, is exactly what makes it impossible to encounter one another. In this mode, every "other" is a threat until we reject the logic of the zero-sum game. Exercises in reflection and meditation that help strip away externalities to find a truer core develop not only our sense of self but also that of others; psychological studies show that the more we have a grasp on our own feelings, the more accurate we are at guessing what others are experiencing.[16]

Creating this kind of mutual recognition and community involved many different kinds of activities—physical, social, and spiritual—in our meetings both before and after beginning the Camino. In the seminar setting before we set off on the Camino, we used meditation and reflective writing along with group reflections designed to tamp down the influence of corrosive Rousseau's self-esteem exemplified in a culture of trying to garner and measure social media "likes." On the Camino, we met at the end of every day to engage in the Ignatian *examen* of the day's walk as a group. On our pre-Camino miniretreat, we used an exercise to present and listen to each other's personal stories and used the tool of the Enneagram to explore our temperaments and particular struggles. The value here is that recognizing oneself in a type is a form of acceptance of one's difference as difference and not imperfection. This spreads to others; their differences are (some of them at least) emotionally basic, not measurements of distance from or failures to

---

16. Lisette van der Meer, Sergi Costafreda, André Aleman, and Anthony S. David, "Self-Reflection and the Brain: A Theoretical Review and Meta-analysis of Neuroimaging Studies with Implications for Schizophrenia," *Neuroscience and Biobehavioral Reviews* 34, no. 6 (May 2010): 935–46, https://www.sciencedirect.com/science/article/pii/S014976340900195X?casa_token=Ch-YDKT_9sAAAAA: ZxPFb6v5xbdzkJdvdp5MBrmx_8Sziz7D5bueZlOZ_epentDUjqblnO8knTMJSSBseVii_iyVSSM.

reach *the* correct/right way to be, leading to a sense that we begin from different strengths and weaknesses and have our own journeys toward integration and stability, ones that will look different for others than for oneself. On the Camino, we set up a structure for grouping, separating, and regrouping as we walked, as those who arrived first for a morning or a lunch break had to wait for those who were walking more slowly. That it was sometimes hard to navigate (as I noted above) doesn't mean the group failed; rather, we were enacting the tension between being a self and being for others, following our own paces and preferences while varying them to fall into step with others, ultimately realizing that we needed the others to have our "own" journey. In the end, most students self-consciously varied their pace, sometimes walking with the slower (or injured) ones, sometimes heading out from a break first and at a faster pace, sometimes alone, and sometimes with a larger group.

Act 3: The Whole World as Place of Exile

One of Rousseau's attempted solutions to the problem of social relations is the creation of homogeneous communities, which can achieve a unified, general will, where all the edges of difference are shaved off, and there is no conflict of wills because all will the same thing.[17] Interestingly, there is a similar sort of picture of the ideal community in Anselm of Canterbury's notion of heaven (to be mirrored as closely as possible in the monastic community) as a place in which I will to will what you will (and vice versa), and all will what God wills. Anselm was well known for expressing extravagant love and this kind of unity of wills for fellow monks, explaining that he

17. This view is put forward in Rousseau's *The Social Contract*.

felt exactly the same extravagant love for all the monks indiscriminately, a "solution" all found disappointing.[18]

Little more than a century later than Anselm, Hugh of Saint Victor confronted the same problem in his *Soliloquy on the Betrothal Gift of the Soul*, which explores the soul's desire to be loved uniquely and exclusively for and as itself.[19] Hugh does not try to redirect or sublimate the desire for a particular love but rather tries to show how it is fulfilled in God's love. The actions and relationship to Jesus Christ are explained in terms of particular love: "Your spouse, your lover, your redeemer, your God, chose and preferred you. He chose you among all and took you up from all and loved you in preference to all."[20] Only then is the soul satisfied, replying, "God does nothing else except provide for my salvation, and he seems to me so completely occupied with guarding me that he forgets all others and chooses to be occupied with me alone."[21]

One of my students described the Camino as somewhere between "all roads lead to Rome" and "my way or the highway," and I think for mere humans, the Camino, like life, is a negotiation between extremes and compromises. However, what Hugh envisions as a divine relationship is one that transcends these tensions and oppositions. I had always understood Hugh's description of the final stage, in which "all the world is a place of exile," as the ultimate rejection of the world, which, for all its allures and beauty, is unsatisfying. But I came to see that it is not just the world's failure but also the comparison to a different, better world, which, once glimpsed, makes our world fall away.

---

18. See Eileen C. Sweeney, *Anselm of Canterbury and the Desire for the Word* (Washington, DC: Catholic University of American Press, 2011), 52–60.
19. Hugh of St. Victor, *Soliloquy on the Betrothal Gift of the Soul*, in *On Love: A Selection of Works of Hugh, Adam, Achard, Richard and Godfrey of St. Victor*, ed. and trans. Hugh Feiss, OSB (New York: New City Press, 2012), sec. 21, p. 210.
20. Hugh, sec. 50, p. 219.
21. Hugh, sec. 65, p. 226.

Our moment where the world fell away occurred at the pilgrim Mass in the beautiful chapel in O'Cebreiro. The simple service was moving, as volunteers speaking different languages stepped forward to do the readings, emphasizing difference and commonality—all of us there from many places and backgrounds but understanding one another across and underneath linguistic barriers. Toward the end of the service, the priest asked everyone to step out of the pews and come up around the altar, and at the final blessing, he started moving from person to person, hugging each one and giving them a small painted rock. I gasped: was he going to hug every single person here? (There were probably seventy to eighty people.) He did. By about halfway through, most had tears streaming down their faces. One of my students wrote about this experience in her final paper and concluded, "Out of this web of human unity stretches the bright line of identity." It was as if Anselm's extravagant love for a particular monk, or God's love for the soul in its uniqueness, was given to each one fully and individually, not generically; it was, for a moment, a world of both/and, not either/or. This student went on to quote Thomas Merton, where he describes coming to a revelatory glimpse of "the depths of our hearts, where neither sin nor desire nor self-knowledge can reach, the core of our reality, the person that each one is in God's eyes." "If only we could all see ourselves as we really are," Merton continues, "if only we could see each other that way all the time," but, he adds, "there is no way of telling people that they are all walking around shining like the sun."[22] For just a moment, this priest told us exactly that, and we felt it about ourselves and each other.

---

22. Thomas Merton, *Conjectures of a Guilty Bystander* (New York: Doubleday, 1966), 140–42.

Epilogue

Even on our Camino, this experience was followed by many more mundane moments, though we remembered it, and it colored the rest of our journey. The bigger challenge by far was to retain it upon return to normal life. One of my students wrote poignantly of his return from the Camino directly into a high-powered internship in New York City. He pictured himself walking in Manhattan with his backpack, rain poncho, and scallop shell symbolizing the Camino and the many paths to its completion, apart from yet among the crowds. Like me and all my students, he is still on the road but with a sense of the world as a place of exile, having glimpsed a sense of a different kind of belonging.

Questions for Reflection

1. How might differences in your group—demographic or individual—impact (enrich/create tensions) the pilgrimage journey? In what sense and to what degree are authentic friendships between members of the group necessary for its success? Are religious identities different than other kinds of identities and/or harder to talk about?

2. Who do you relate to in Chaucer's "types" in terms of seeing either yourself or others you know in them? Do you think examining and using any kind of "personality type" system is useful?

3. Do you experience a tension between authentic experience and "performing" for a grade in a pilgrimage class? How could we attempt to "be" on the pilgrimage as opposed to feeling like it is a series of selfies?

4. Are there dystopic elements of society from which you wish to escape? How do they compare with Rousseau's view of society based on the corrosive effects of self-esteem—the desire to be desired by others?

5. What are the "whats" in your life that you embrace? That you reject? Have you experienced the difference between revealing (and having recognized) the "who" as opposed to the "what" you are?

6. What do you think would be difficult about retaining the insights and the feelings of the intense experience of pilgrimage when you return home? What could you do to retain the insights of the pilgrimage after it is over?

Select Annotated Bibliography

Aristotle. *Nicomachean Ethics*. Translated by Martin Ostwald. Upper Saddle River, NJ: Prentice Hall, 1999.

Book 8 on friendship and book 9, especially chapters 4 and 8–9, describe the different kinds of friendship, the possible conflicts between love of self and love of others, and a notion of self-love modeled on friendship with the self.

Barbezat, Daniel P., and Mirabai Bush. *Contemplative Practices in Higher Education: Powerful Methods to Transform Teaching and Learning*. San Francisco: Jossey-Bass, 2014.

This book contains a wealth of information and exercises for use in the classroom that develop deeper reflection and empathy.

Chaucer, Geoffrey. *The Canterbury Tales*.

Especially the introduction and "The Knight's Tale." The introduction describes the characters on the pilgrimage, and some have been seen as types or even human archetypes.

William Blake's engraving of Chaucer's pilgrims concludes by describing them as "the Physiognomies or Lineaments of Universal Human Life beyond which Nature never steps" (David V. Erdman, ed., *The Complete Poetry and Prose of William Blake*, with commentary by Harold Bloom [New York: Anchor, 1988], 570; you can read Blake's description of his painting at the William Blake Archive: http://www.blakearchive .org/copy/bb32.d?descId=bb32.d.te.01). The knight's tale is relevant, as the story veers back and forth between tragedy and comedy and raises questions about what the real difference is.

Oliver, Mary. Available in many collections and online.

Oliver's poems are especially evocative in the pilgrimage classroom both because she was herself inspired by a lifetime of walking and because the poems are deeply reflective of both joy and pain, written in accessible and direct language. We read "The Journey," "Wild Geese," "Morning Poem," "Song of the Builders," "Bone," and "The Summer Day."

Rohr, Richard, and Andreas Ebert. *The Enneagram: A Christian Perspective*. Translated by Peter Heinegg. New York: Crossroads, 2016.

The enneagram is the typology of nine personality types that goes back to Evagrius Ponticus, a fourth-century Christian mystic. The aim of the enneagram was to know your type in order to know the vices you might be most prone to and to work toward transforming those vices into virtues. See this work by Rohr and Ebert for a deep and historically based understanding.

Rousseau, Jean-Jacques. *Discourse on the Origin and Foundations of Inequality among Men in the Basic Political Writings*. Translated by Donald A. Cress. Indianapolis: Hackett, 1987.

—————. *The Reveries of a Solitary Walker*. Translated by Charles E. Butterworth. Indianapolis, IN: Hackett, 1992.

These two works are psychological and political explorations of solitude, social dystopia, and inequality.

Solnit, Rebecca. *Wanderlust: A History of Walking*. London: Penguin, 2000.

This book contains chapters on city and rural walking from the Greeks, to the Romantic poets, to the surrealists, connecting walking with our social, political, and aesthetic concerns.

Taylor, Barbara Brown. *An Altar in the World: A Geography of Faith*. New York: Harper Collins, 2009.

Taylor's exploration of bodily practices (such as "wearing skin," "getting lost," "feeling pain," "walking the earth" and encountering others) opens up new ways to connect to our physicality and to others that circumvent our embedded Cartesian separation between body and soul and between self and other.

PART 2

Contexts

Chapter 6

India

The Pilgrim People

Yann Vagneux, MEP
Resident scholar and priest, Benares, India
Translated by Jeffrey Bloechl

Those who wish to enter the soul of India cannot be satisfied with the silence of libraries. They must set out toward the vast horizons crossed by countless pilgrimage routes, where, since the dawn of time, a civilization has lived out its inextinguishable quest for the Absolute. Indeed, as far as we go back in time, we can still see the Indian people, with a light step and a joyful heart, stretched toward a mysterious place whose spiritual radiance justifies all the sufferings endured to reach it. Thus, in book 3 of the epic *Mahābhārata*, while Arjuna is in Indra's heaven, his four other Pandavas brothers and their wife Draupadi undertake a visit to the sacred places—*tīrtha*—spread over the four cardinal points. In their wake, generations of Hindus have wandered around the Akhand Bharat, the undivided India stretching from the borders of present-day Pakistan to those of Bangladesh and from Nepal to Sri Lanka.

However, Hindu believers are not the only ones who visit auspicious places, illustrious temples, or famous masters. The whole of India has made pilgrimage one of the most striking realities of their religious practice. Before his final extinction, did not the

Buddha (563–483 BCE) draw a map of the future pilgrimage to the key places of his earthly life, where fifteen centuries later, his disciples continue to go with great fervor? "Ananda, there are four places which the faithful should visit with feelings of reverence and awe. Which are they? 'Here the Tathagata was born' is the first. 'Here the Tathagata attained supreme enlightenment' is the second. 'Here the Tathagata set in motion the Wheel of the Dharma' is the third. 'Here the Tathagata attained *parinirvāṇa* without reminder' is the fourth. And Ananda, the faithful monks and nuns, while making the pilgrimage to these shrines with a devout heart will, at the break-up of the body after death, be reborn in a heavenly world."[1] The eloquent name of "Tathagata" (meaning "thus gone") recalls that the inner awakening of the Buddha has always been accompanied by his intense activity as a traveling preacher.

The Jains, disciples of Mahavira (599–527 BCE), the last of the *tīrthaṅkaras*, or "ford makers," also have their pilgrimages, the most famous of which are at Palitana in Gujarat and Shikharji in Jharkhand. At the top of these sacred mountains, where the *tīrthaṅkaras* once meditated and obtained ultimate deliverance, the faithful come to immerse themselves in an ancestral spiritual experience that gives them a unique identity in the multireligious Indian landscape. Iconically, the Jain monks live a life of continual wandering on the roads so that no external attachments hinder their inner liberation.

Since Islam came to India in the eighth century, Muslims have made Al-Hind, or Hindustan, a sacred land covered with *dargahs*, the tombs of Sufi masters, the most famous of which is that of Moinuddin Chishti (1141–1236 BCE) in Ajmer, where tens of thousands of pilgrims flock daily. Dear to the hearts of the Sikhs—a

---

1. *Mahāparinibbāna Sutta* 5:8, in *The Long Discourses of the Buddha: A Translation of the "Digha Nikaya,"* trans. M. Walshe (Somerville: Wisdom, 1995), 263–64.

spiritual path born in the wake of Guru Nanak (1469–1539 CE)—are the Golden Temple of Amritsar or Hemkund Sahib, a lake located at an elevation of over 4,600 meters in the Himalayas. As for the Christians, they also have established several shrines across the country, and it is moving to meet them at the end of August walking for days to reach the Basilica of Velankanni, often called the "Lourdes of South India."

Finally, there are pilgrimages common to several religions, such as the fabled Mount Kailash. This resplendent summit in perfect solitude on the Tibetan plateau is the object of the ultimate desire of Hindus, Bonpos, Buddhists, and Jains, who circumambulate the "snow jewel" to better take in its intense spiritual presence. A fellow pilgrim of the sacred mountain, Raimundo Panikkar (1918–2010), wrote, "Kailash is a temple of the Absolute. Unlike all mosques, cathedrals or temples, it is not made by man. Kailash simply *is*, it is there. It was *discovered* as . . . a sacred symbol for all who recognize it and, by recognizing it, invest the mountain with a new degree of reality."[2]

Tīrthayātrā

While pilgrimage is a reality common to all Indian religions, I would like to focus more particularly on the way it is lived at the heart of Hindu traditions. The importance of a single Sanskrit word is immediately obvious: *tīrthayātrā*. Derived from the verbal root describing displacement, *yātrā* means "the journey," but composed with the term *tīrtha*, it precisely designates pilgrimage. As for *tīrtha*, it originally designated fording or crossing a river, but then the term took on a deeper meaning to indicate the blessed place leading to the

---

2. Raimundo Panikkar, *Pèlerinage au Kailash. Retour à la Source* (Paris: Le Cerf, 2011), 18.

further spiritual shore of the world. In her remarkable book devoted to the sacred geography of India precisely formed by the dense network of places of pilgrimage, Diana Eck has written, "The *tīrtha* is a place of spiritual crossing, where the gods are close and the benefits of worship generous. At a spiritual crossing place, one's prayers are amplified, one's rites are more efficacious, one's vows more readily fulfilled."[3] For a Hindu, *tīrthayātrā* is a pilgrimage to the sources of sacred rivers, their confluences (*saṅgama*), and their mouths into the ocean. It is also a pilgrimage to the great temples, such as the one leading to the four sanctuaries of Puri in the east, Rameswaram in the south, Dwarka in the west, and Badrinath in the north—shrines that, when visited, provide liberation (*mokṣa*) from the cycle of rebirth. It is remarkable to find the spiritual description of the Indian *tīrthas* in a text as old as the *Skanda Purāṇa* (eighth century), which could be considered the ancestor of our contemporary Lonely Planet travel books! In the style proper to the *māhātmyas* (praises), the glory of sacred places is celebrated abundantly, and the myths associated with them are remembered. These documents have survived the centuries and continue to be the subject of popular publications that are available at the entrance of the *tīrthas*. Finally, to the various places giving rise to a *yātrā* we must add those that are blessed by the presence of a guru still living in his body or having already left it—in particular the ashrams. Here, another Sanskrit term is essential to capture the holiness of those different places: *darshan*, or vision (*darśana* in Sanskrit). Indeed, when a Hindu undertakes a pilgrimage, it is to come into the presence of the divine and contemplate it, as it is revealed as much in the heart of the temples as in the radiant faces of the spiritual masters. *Darshan* is, so to speak, the keystone of the entire

---

3. Diana Eck, *India: A Sacred Geography* (New York: Harmony, 2012), 7.

spiritual quest of Hinduism.[4] Obtaining the desired *darshan* also means receiving, for oneself or for one's ancestors, some *puṇyas*, or merits that will promote a more lenient existence in the next life.

The term *tīrthayātrā* thus recalls that since the dawn of time, the vitality of Hinduism has been manifested in countless pilgrimages. This is still the case today in a religion that, for more than fifteen centuries, has been transfigured by the *bhakti*, or the path of devotion. I could cite here many poems composed by the great figures of this tradition, such as those of Tukaram (1598–1649 CE), which are still sung by pilgrims on the way from Pandharpur to Maharashtra. In addition, with the development of air transport and the enrichment of the middle class, pilgrimages have recently experienced an upsurge, even if the fervor of the crowds is now sometimes taken over by the fundamentalist drift of a certain political Hinduism. In the joyous community-building experience that unites all generations (even if the elders have more time for the *yātrās*) and all strata of society, everyone can reclaim the religious identity that is so intimately linked to a land sanctified by the uninterrupted prayer of generations of Hindus. How unforgettable is the great bath of February 10, 2013, during the Kumbha Mela in Prayagraj (Allahabad), where, in a few hours, more than thirty-five million people plunged into the confluence of the Ganges and the Yamuna! We then understand that at the end of their pilgrimage, believers feel renewed and capable of resuming the course of their daily existence, always keeping in their hearts the divine light of the *darshan* received.

In these innumerable *yātrās*, the Hindus discover the pilgrim form of existence that I might dare to say is a key to understanding this religion. Along the way, it is not surprising to meet young

---

4. See Diana Eck, *Darśan: Seeing the Divine Image in India* (New York: Columbia University Press, 1998).

engineers from Bangalore, living at the forefront of high tech, who have for a time decided to strip themselves of the comforts of their lives in order to embrace, as do the humblest of their people, the precarious condition of the pilgrim, which is also that of the wandering monk, or *saṃnyāsin*. After having renounced their family and any position in society, these itinerant hermits, draped in their long saffron robes, engage in holy wandering, or *parivrāja*, in order to avoid any earthly attachment. Depending on the dates of religious festivals or the alternation of the seasons, they can be found either in the burning plains or in the Himalayas. Along the way, they take possession of India's "sacred geography" and share the age-old wisdom of their tradition. The words of the Jesuit Michel de Certeau apply perfectly to these men who are guided by the Spirit, of whom "we do not know where he comes from or where he is going" (John 3:8): "The one who is mystical is one who cannot stop walking and who, with the certainty of what he lacks, knows from every place and every object that it is not that, that one cannot reside here, nor be satisfied with that."[5]

Toward the Source

As a Catholic priest consecrated to India, I have often mingled with crowds of pilgrims in order to enter more deeply into the spiritual quest of my chosen people and to share their joy in entering the presence of the divine in the spiritual high places. In particular, during many summers, I went to the shrines of Uttarakhand, following in the footsteps of Swami Abhishiktananda (Henri Le Saux, 1910–73) and his disciple Swami Ajatananda (Marc Chaduc, 1944–77). The two French monks lived in these places, on

---

5. Michel de Certeau, *La Fable mystique* (Paris: Gallimard, 1982), 411.

the banks of the Ganges, which originates in the Himalayas. Both had grasped the importance of what Hindus call the *devbhūmi*, the "land of the gods" blessed among all, "because that land carries a mystery—and an ever-powerful mystery—the very one that radiates from the hearts of the sages who are engulfed there, some who disappear forever from human memory, buried in the most inaccessible retreats amongst the rocks, in the asceticism, and even more in the awakening."[6] Of Uttarakhand, literally the "land of the north," the poet Kalidasa (fifth century) declared, in the first verse of his *Kumārasaṃbhavam*, that "the mystery of the gods resides in the north in the supreme abode of the Himalayas of unsurpassable grandeur" (my translation). Before contemplating the splendor of the *devbhūmi*, I learned to love it by reading the stories that Abhishiktananda and Ajatananda left us: "The crowds of India set off each year on pilgrimage to visit the famous sanctuaries of the Himalayas, High Kailash and the sources of the Ganges. It is the universal response of man to the call which comes from the hills whose summits he instinctively connects with the dwelling place of God, his Creator. And irresistibly, he returns there as if to the source of his being. Down from those heights flow both the streams which water the earth and also those mystical rivers to which souls come to find the water of life."[7]

The pilgrimage to the source of the Ganges is one of the most famous in India. It is performed by hundreds of thousands of people each year from the end of April until the festival of Diwali in October–November. It begins at Haridwar, where the Ganges enters the plain, and for more than a thousand kilometers, it leads

6. Ajatananda, *Terre sacrée. L'Uttarakhand et ses mystères* (unpublished text), April 12, 1976.

7. Abhishiktananda, *The Mountain of the Lord: Pilgrimage to Gangotri* (Bangalore: Christian Institute for the Study of Religion and Society, 1966), 1.

A pilgrim on the way to the source of the Ganges. Photo by the author.

to the four temples of Yamunotri (source of the Yamuna River), Gangotri (source of the Bhagirathi River, one of the main affluents of the Ganges), Kedarnath (shrine dedicated to Shiva), and Badrinath (shrine dedicated to Vishnu). In the time of Abhishiktananda and Ajatananda, it was carried out over several weeks while facing the many dangers of the Himalayan solitude. It is now reduced to eight days by car and even less for those who take a helicopter. Only a few monks retain the original spirit of patient walking—the *padyātrā*. For twenty years, the Char Dham pilgrimage[8] has continued to attract more and more crowds, causing terrible human and ecological tragedies, as seen during the terrible floods of Kedarnath in June 2013, which claimed the lives of more than ten thousand

---

8. *Char Dham* means "the four shrines," hence the name of the Himalayan pilgrimage.

people. Finally, it is remarkable to note that for the Indians, it is more important to go back to the source of the sacred river than to go to its mouth in the ocean, located at Gangasagar in the south of Calcutta. This expresses a spiritual teaching that is of great importance to understand.

Among the many pilgrimages I have made in Uttarakhand, I have a special attachment to the one to Gangotri, benefiting from the friendship of the Semwal Brahmin priests who serve this holy place. I love to accompany them for the opening of the shrine on the auspicious day of *Akṣayā tritiya*, the third day of the month of Vaiśakha (April–May). From the Haridwar railway station, I catch a bus that brings me to Uttarkashi, the "Benares (Kashi) of the north," on the banks of the Bhagirathi River, which, together with the Alakananda and Mandakini Rivers, form the Ganges farther downstream at Devprayag. On the second day, another bus takes me to Mukhba, a small village where the Semwal Brahmins come from. This is the place where the statue of the goddess Ganga resides during the six months of winter when the temple of Gangotri is closed. On the eve of *Akṣayā tritiya*, the priests set out to accompany on foot the goddess's palanquin (enclosed litter) for twenty kilometers, bringing her, too, on pilgrimage back up to her temple. It is a sight of great beauty, facing the snowcapped peaks and along the blossoming apple trees. The Brahmins are overjoyed at the prospect of resuming their ancestral service of Ma Ganga, their benevolent mother. Throughout the procession, horns echo in the valley, as do the joyful songs of the faithful. The night is spent in prayer in the freezing cold of Bhaironghati. The next day at dawn, the march resumes with redoubled enthusiasm at the idea of reaching Gangotri very soon. Already the courtyards of the temple have been lavishly decorated with garlands of flowers, and many pilgrims await the arrival of the goddess. Her entry is a real triumph. Then begins a long liturgy of several hours to honor Ma Ganga according to a royal ceremony during which she is ritually awakened, bathed, dressed, adorned, and fed, all accompanied by the recitation of the Vedas. Then her golden statue is taken to the heart of the shrine, where, in the middle of the day, she gives her first *darshan* to the joyful crowds.

For Hindus, Gangotri is the place where the goddess Ganga—who until then flowed in the sky in the form of the Milky Way—came down to earth in favorable response to the harsh penance performed by Prince Bhagiratha, who begged her to come to purify the ashes of the sixty thousand sons of Sagar, his distant ancestors. During the evening ceremony of the Arati, when the Ganges is venerated with an offering of light, incense, and flowers, the myth of her saving descent is recalled by the faithful: "O Goddess Ganga! You are the divine river from heaven, you are the savior of all the three worlds, you are pure and restless, you adorn Lord Shiva's head. O Mother! May my mind always rest at your lotus feet."[9] In Gangotri, the pilgrims' day begins early with a purifying bath in the Ganges, which in this place is a rushing torrent. Then they take their turn to enter the temple. And then, after having bought plastic or brass containers, they fill them in the sacred flows and ask the priests to perform a special prayer (*pūjā*) to invoke a divine blessing on this water, which will later be used in family rituals, such as those associated with the dead. The pilgrims then enter their names in carefully preserved registers, where they can find traces of the arrival of their forefathers. The day passes in great religious fervor—everyone being aware of receiving maternal protection from the goddess Ganga: "O Jahnavi! O Ganga! Your waters flowing through the Himalayas make you even more beautiful. You are

9. Adi Shankaracarya, *Śri Ganga Stotram*, Chinmaya Mission Chicago, accessed March 28, 2022, https://www.mychinmaya.org/bv/bvresources/gangastotram.pdf, 1.

the daughter of the silent sages. You are savior of the people fallen from their path, and so you are revered in all three worlds."[10]

The geographic source of the river is at Gaumukh, eighteen kilometers upstream. Relatively few people go that far because the merits of the pilgrimage (*punya*) are obtained in the Gangotri temple. Land of the hermits, Gaumukh—literally "the mouth of the cow"—is a glacial cavity from which the river Bhagirathi surges, at the foot of the dazzling peaks of the Bhagirathis (6,856 m) and the Shivling (6,543 m), rising like a perfect pillar in a single line from its base to the top. In its extreme nakedness, it is one of the most awe-inspiring places in India, filling those who come before it with emotion. Here pilgrims contemplate the pure beauty of beginnings that powerfully reveals the presence of the divine. Some are not afraid to bathe in icy waters to commune even more deeply with the emergence of the sacred river. Then they stand silently on the shore, as if drawn into greater depths—those of their own hearts. I, too, like to remain for a long time in front of the source. Then alone, but intimately united in prayer to my Hindu brothers and sisters, I celebrate the Eucharist in continuity with the Mass that Swami Abhishiktananda and Raimundo Panikkar held in this place on June 6, 1964, "hidden in a hollow among the rocks a few steps away from the stream, whilst the sound of water rushing over the boulders provided a mighty organ."[11] I performed this rite in their spirit: "The bread and wine which I shall offer in my Mass will be the call to God of all these pilgrims at the sacred sources of rivers in the Himalayas, of all the priests, all ascetics, those of our time, of days gone by and of the future, for the Eucharist transcends all time."[12]

---

10. Shankaracarya, 5.
11. Letter from Henri Le Saux to Marie-Thérèse Le Saux, June 28, 1964, in *Vers l'expérience intérieure*, by H. Le Saux (Paris: Artège-Lethielleux, 2018), 182.
12. Abhishiktananda, *Mountain of the Lord*, 33.

An Inner Pilgrimage

Back in the plains, following the course of the Ganges toward Benares, where I reside, I cherish the memory of the people of Gangotri: the devotional service performed by the Brahmins, the merry groups of pilgrims crowding the riverbank, and the unspeakable peace transmitted by silent renunciates. The grace of the pilgrimage is collected in me, and it seems to me that it is deepening. Benares is also one of the most revered places in India. The holy city reproduces in microcosm the sacred geography of the country with its great sanctuaries.[13] Thus, to go to the temples of Benares is to obtain the same merits as if one went to the four cardinal points of the subcontinent. And beyond the pilgrimage, when one sets out to accomplish a long journey, there is another pilgrimage, interior and motionless, that is above all part of what Hinduism calls a *sādhanā*, or a spiritual exercise. This is why many friends in Benares advise me not to go far away but instead to remain quiet in the holy city and take the only path that matters: that of descent to the depths of the heart. This is precisely what Adi Shankara (788–820 CE) sang when revealing how much Benares, traditionally called Kashi, with its cremation pyres at Manikarnika Ghat, is the very sacrament of inner awakening:

> *The rest of the mind is peace supreme,*
> *And that is Manikarnika, the greatest place of pilgrimage.*
> *The stream of wisdom is the pure, original Ganges.*
> *I am that Kashi whose essence is self-knowledge.*

---

13. See Diana Eck, *Banaras: City of Light* (Princeton, NJ: Princeton University Press, 1983).

In Kashi the light shines.
That light illuminates everything.
Whoever knows that light, truly reaches Kashi.

The body is the sacred field of Kashi.
All-pervading wisdom is the Ganges, Mother of the Three
  Worlds. . . .
If all this dwells within my body,
What other place of pilgrimage can there be?[14]

Basically, we could say that Benares is the end of any pilgrimage, or rather the beginning of the only pilgrimage that is truly worth accomplishing: "The mind of those who have beheld Kashi delights no more in other tirthas."[15]

At its mystical heights, the quest of Hinduism is a pilgrimage from what passes to what eternally remains. It is a response to the call to origins that leads back, far away from every cosmic manifestation. "Success to you in crossing beyond darkness!"[16] sings the *Muṇḍaka Upaniṣad*, and the *Bṛhadāraṇyaka Upaniṣad* details the stages of the inner journey: "From the unreal lead me to the real. From darkness lead me to light. From death lead me to immortality."[17] Yet we are so immersed in the opacity of everyday life that we sometimes need the blessed time of an outer pilgrimage to be led back to the original source from which all existence comes to the "Invisible called the Everlasting."[18] Such is the ultimately interior journey toward the divine origin from which we do not return,

14. Adi Shankaracarya, *Kâśī Pañcakaṃ* 1, 4, 5, trans. Diana Eck, in Eck, *Banaras*, 302.
15. *Kāśī Rahasya* 13, 54–55, trans. Diana Eck, in Eck, *Banaras*, 305.
16. *Muṇḍaka Upaniṣad* II, 2, 6, in *The Upanisads*, trans. Valerie Roebuck (London: Penguin, 2003), 326.
17. *Bṛhadāraṇyaka Upaniṣad* I, 3, 28, in Roebuck, *Upanisads*, 19.
18. *Bhagavadgītā* VIII, 21, in *Bhavagad Gita*, trans. Juan Mascaró (London: Penguin, 1968), 79.

because, as proclaimed by the *Chāndogya Upaniṣad* in its final cry, "na ca punar āvartate na ca punar āvartate" (and [he] does not return—and does not return!).[19]

We then understand why in India the *saṃnyāsin* is the guardian of the true spirit of the pilgrimage. Whether he is engaged in endless wandering in order to be detached from any bond or instead remains motionless in the concentration of body and mind, he is dedicated to unique spiritual work: to pierce "the mystery of Glory and immortality, raised to the highest heavens, hidden in the secret of the heart, where only those who have renounced everything can penetrate."[20] The ascetic then no longer needs to speak, because the silent teaching that he offers is an invitation to all to descend to the depths of their being. The place where he dwells is the cave of the heart—the *guhā* in Sanskrit—in which one descends into the depths of the darkness in order to then ascend to the highest of the dazzling lights.[21] "Pilgrim to the source of the Ganges, it is within myself that I climb up to the ineffable attainment of the Source of Being,"[22] wrote Swami Ajatananda in 1976, when undertaking a three-month *yātrā* to the shrines of Uttarakhand, in the footsteps of his master, Swami Abhishiktananda. The cave of Gaumukh at the source of the Ganges then reveals all its powerful symbolism—that of the definitive completion of any pilgrimage:

At the very center of being,
at the source of the heart,
at the very depth of myself
where I myself die

---

19. *Chāndogya Upaniṣad* VIII, 15, in Roebuck, *Upanisads*, 204.
20. *Mahānārāyaṇa Upaniṣad* XII, 14 (translation mine).
21. Cf. *Kaṭha Upaniṣad* III, 1, "Having entered the secret place and the utmost height" (*guhāṃ praviṣṭau parame parārdhe*), in Roebuck, *Upanisads*, 281.
22. Ajatananda, *Terre sacrée*, prologue.

something shines
unique and solitary
without any other sign except oneself
lost in the Mystery.[23]

Questions for Reflection

1. In India, pilgrimage is an essential expression of popular devotion prevalent in Hinduism but also in Islam, Sikhism, Jainism, and Christianity. The deeply communal experience of pilgrimage allows each one to be personally strengthened in their religious identity. How does the pilgrimage experience also constitute your own renewal of faith and belonging?

2. The famous Tibetan hermit Milarepa (1052–1135 CE) affirmed, "You always flee elsewhere, but the desire for freedom is illusory. So remain here to destroy the illusions of your mind."[24] His abrupt words show that the pilgrimage is above all an inner journey. How does the pilgrimage experience enable you to accomplish this ascent to the depths of your heart?

3. Believers unite their steps with those of believers of other religions, making a pilgrimage with them. Even if they do not share the same faith, they share deeply in their joy and are enriched spiritually by their fervor. How can you let the other's religious experience amaze and teach you?

---

23. Ajatananda, *Terre sacrée*, 10–11.
24. See Milarépa, *La vie: Les cent mille chants*, trans. Marie-José Lamothe (Paris: Fayard, 2006).

Select Annotated Bibliography

Abhishiktananda. *The Mountain of the Lord: Pilgrimage to Gangotri*. Bangalore: Christian Institute for the Study of Religion and Society, 1966.

The iconic book of the French monk relating his pilgrimage to the sources of the Ganges with Raimundo Panikkar in 1964.

Alter, Stephen. *Sacred Waters: A Pilgrimage of the Ganges River to the Source of Hindu Culture*. Boston: Houghton Mifflin Harcourt, 2001.

The book recounts Stephen Alter's journey along the ancient pilgrim paths toward the sources of the Ganges at the end of the 1990s.

Eck, Diana. *India: A Sacred Geography*. New York: Harmony, 2012.

The classic study on the networks of pilgrimages in India by one of its foremost scholars.

Gaullier, Tanneguy. *L'âme du Gange: Un pèlerinage aux sources*. Paris: Transboréal, 2016.

The travelogue of a French man who walked all along the Ganges from its mouth back to the source.

Sax, William. *Mountain Goddess: Gender and Politics in a Himalayan Pilgrimage*. New York: Oxford University Press, 1991.

A comprehensive study of the famous pilgrimage of the goddess Nanda Devi occurring every twelve years in the Indian Himalayas.

Vagneux, Yann. *Indian Portraits: Eight Christian Encounters with Hinduism*. New Delhi: Nirala, 2021.

Among the eight Christian encounters with Hinduism, the lives in India of Abhishiktananda (Henri Le Saux) and his disciple Ajatananda (Marc Chaduc) are described.

———. *A Priest in Banaras*. Bangalore: Asian Trading, 2020.

The holy city of India and its spiritual heritage seen through the eyes of a Catholic priest living along the Ganges.

Chapter 7

Pilgrimage and Pedagogy

Muslim-Christian Perspectives and Contemporary Practices

Albertus Bagus Laksana, SJ
*President of Sanata Dharma University,
Yogyakarta, Indonesia*

Always Formative and Pedagogical

Pilgrimage and Spiritual Formation

Le Grand Voyage (2004; written and directed by Ismaël Ferroukhi) is an unusual movie on a pilgrimage journey to Mecca done by a father and his son, Reda, a young boy of French-Moroccan descent. The two live under the same roof but do not understand each other. It is very interesting that this story mirrors the stories of its director, Ferroukhi, and perhaps many others. Ferroukhi sees the film as about spirituality rather than religion, "about what's behind appearances, and how to break down barriers." He is quoted as saying, "I was trying to make silence eloquent, because the deepest things are conveyed without words."[1] In this movie, silence has become a way of forging deeper communication among the pilgrims (father and son) but also between pilgrims and their own selves, the cosmos, and God.

---

1. Maya Jaggi, "The Long and Winding Road," *Guardian*, October 7, 2005, https://www
.theguardian.com/film/2005/oct/07/1.

In the movie, the father and son must learn to reconnect while driving in an old car along the three-thousand-mile, ten-country route from southern France to Saudi Arabia. It is in this intense journey that communication and intergenerational gaps must be dealt with, maybe for the first time. In the first place, Reda and his father won't speak the same language. Reda insists on speaking only French, while his father sticks to Arabic despite his mastery of French. Furthermore, the young and secular Reda wants to have a sightseeing experience, while his religious father insists on the sacred goal of the journey.

The movie is a contemporary rendition of the hajj, a canonical pilgrimage of Muslims to the holy city of Mecca. However, it also emphasizes that this hajj is a real and rich journey rather than just a performance of a ritual. It is done by concrete persons who live in a certain societal context with real-life struggles, and who are in search of diverse things. However, at the end, what really matters is the things that concern their spiritual well-being. When Reda asks him why he would not just fly to Mecca, which is so much more practical, his father replies, "When the waters of the ocean rise to the heavens, they lose their bitterness to become pure again; the ocean waters evaporate when they rise to the clouds, and as they evaporate, they become fresh." As illustrated by the movie, this pilgrimage journey opens different avenues for encounters of all kinds, which is made possible because the souls are purified of distractions. It is a journey where silence and solitude become a sine qua non condition for meaningful encounter with the other, where pilgrims get sidetracked at times but eventually get back to the right direction, where they receive a visit by "strangers" (a mysterious woman and man), and where important decisions about life itself are made. At the end of the movie, the father dies in Mecca. Death during the hajj is considered the noblest culmination of the whole journey. And for Reda, witnessing the moment of his father's death left an important mark on his spiritual transformation in relation to God and his father.

In a nutshell, this movie portrays pilgrimage (and religion in general) as a means of purification and a pedagogy of the heart. This is in line with the idea of religion as a pedagogy of desire geared toward weaning humanity from idolatry.[2] To a large extent, the practice of pilgrimage in general has always been pedagogical. It educates, and even cures, the soul. And true pilgrimage always involves a degree of spiritual purification and growth. So pilgrimage is an integral mode of piety. Even the quest for particular blessings (Ar. *baraka*) in pilgrimage demands to be placed within a larger spiritual quest that involves a deeper and more personal learning experience. That is why the process, or the journey, is crucial. As *Le Grand Voyage* illustrates, the route is as important as the destination, for it enables the formative and fruitful interaction between space and time, between exteriority and interiority, and between the self and otherness in the life contexts of the pilgrims and their communities.

Pilgrimage and the Search for Knowledge

Spiritual experience and diverse forms of knowledge, such as knowledge of otherness, of other cultures and language, have been involved in the dynamics of both Muslim and Christian pilgrimage. The following is the way Ali ibn Abi Bakr al-Harawi (d. 611 H/1215 CE), a curious and avid Muslim pilgrim who spent most of his life in Syria summarized his life as a pilgrim: "I roam the lands east and west; to many a wanderer and hermit was I a companion. I saw every strange and marvelous wonder, and experienced terror

---

2. Nicholas Lash, "Criticism or Construction? The Task of the Theologian," in *Theology on the Way to Emmaus* (London: SCM, 1986), 3–17.

in comfort and misery. I have to come to be buried alone beneath the earth; I hope that my Lord will be my companion."[3] Using contemporary images, *Le Grand Voyage* illustrates this dynamic of communication and learning as well, as it "becomes a film about language and communication across gulfs of faith, culture and generation, between migrant and second-generation beurs, orthodox and non-believer."[4]

In the Islamic tradition, the search for knowledge in the context of pilgrimage is emphasized. The hajj, for example, is a canonical pilgrimage that often involves a prolonged period of religious learning in the company of scholars in centers of Islamic wisdom.[5] The Muslim tradition has also been graced with paradigmatic pilgrim-cum-travelers, such as Ibn Batuta and al-Harawi, who combined the search for knowledge of all kinds with pious visitation of holy places, including those belonging to different religious traditions and cultures, where sacredness and the presence of God were encountered in unfamiliar ways. This genre of spiritual travel is called *rihla*, and it also functions as a means of forging the traveler's identity.[6]

In the earliest phase of Christian pilgrimage to the Holy Land, religious curiosity and the search for knowledge was an important motif as well. Egeria, the famous woman pilgrim of the ancient world, was driven by curiosity (*satis curiosa*) and demanded that things

---

3. Josef W. Meri, *A Lonely Wayfarer's Guide to Pilgrimage: 'Ali ibn Abi Bakr al-Harawi's "Kitab al-isharat ila Ma'rifat al-Ziyarat"* (Princeton, NJ: Darwin, 2004), xxv.

4. Jaggi, "Long and Winding Road." *Beur* is a French word designating European-born people whose parents or grandparents are immigrants from the Maghreb.

5. Cf. Eric Tagliacozzo, *The Longest Journey: Southeast Asians and the Pilgrimage to Mecca* (Oxford: Oxford University Press, 2013); Venetia Porter, ed., *The Hajj: Journey to the Heart of Islam* (Cambridge, MA: Harvard University Press, 2012); and Robert R. Bianchi, *The Guests of God: Pilgrimage and Politics in the Islamic World* (Oxford: Oxford University Press, 2004).

6. See, for example, Kennet Garden, "The *rihla* and Self-Reinvention of Abū Bakr Ibn al-'Arabī," *Journal of the American Oriental Society* 135, no. 1 (January–March 2015): 1–17.

should be shown to her "according to the Scriptures." Pilgrims wanted to be informed about the things they saw.[7] That is why pilgrims also studied the Bible as preparation. However, the fact that Egeria felt the need to compose rather detailed reports on her pilgrimage journey to her circle also shows the deeper connection between knowledge and religious affection. Explaining why she reported on the liturgical celebrations in Jerusalem, she wrote, "So that your affection should know what is the daily process in the holy places day by day, it has become my duty to inform you from my knowledge, because you would be glad to know these things."[8]

Lessons from the Masters: Ignatius of Loyola and Abu Hamid al-Ghazali

To illustrate the relationship among pilgrimage, the search for knowledge, and spiritual pedagogy, it is insightful to compare two figures: the Muslim scholar Abu Hamid al-Ghazali (1058–1111) and the Catholic saint Ignatius of Loyola (1491–1556). In the pilgrimage journeys of these two paradigmatic figures, we see a fruitful combination of a spiritual quest and the search for knowledge, or pedagogy for the soul and pedagogy for the mind.

In the case of Saint Ignatius, the pilgrimage journey began with a personal crisis in the aftermath of the Battle of Pamplona (1521). A physical wound shattered his worldly dreams of fame and success and eventually led to a journey of spiritual transformation and the quest for knowledge (theology and spirituality) in Paris. Ignatius's pilgrimage involved physical journeys along a route of

---

7. Pierre Maraval, "The Earliest Phase of Christian Pilgrimage in the Near East (before the 7th Century)," *Dumbarton Oaks Papers* 56 (2002): 72.

8. *Itinerarium Egeriae* (IE) 24.1, in Hagith Sivan, "Holy Land Pilgrimage and Western Audiences: Some Reflections on Egeria and Her Circle," *Classical Quarterly* 38, no. 2 (1988): 530.

transformation and penitence, where he visited Marian shrines and other holy places in northern Spain (the shrines of Aránzazu and Montserrat), where he went into seclusion (the cave of Manresa), where he sought conversations with spiritual persons (e.g., in Manresa and Barcelona), and where he dealt with spiritual ailments and physical sickness.[9] Ignatius's journey was also marked by the search for diverse kinds of knowledge. He was granted mystical inner knowledge at the bank of the river Cardoner and also on other occasions during the journey.

Regarding the longer dynamic of Saint Ignatius's pilgrimage, one can say that it is a pilgrimage that led to another pilgrimage. He thought of doing a pilgrimage as soon as he realized his need for personal transformation. Then quite early in his spiritual journey of conversion, he felt the desire for another pilgrimage—namely, to go to the Holy Land and stay there to win souls for God. He managed to go to the Holy Land as a pilgrim but failed in his intention to work there. This failure led to his awareness that he needed to undergo academic study to be a better instrument for God's work. After finishing his studies in Paris, together with his first companions, he again attempted a (failed) plan to work in Jerusalem, a center of Christian pilgrimage; instead, they went to Rome to make themselves available for the pope's mission.[10] In a way, the Society of Jesus, which Saint Ignatius and his early companions founded, was born due to these failed pilgrimages. Within the mission of the Jesuit order, other centers and forms of pilgrimage emerged: the whole world, rather than just the Holy Land, would be the arena for this new kind of pilgrimage journey connected to apostolic mission.

---

9. Saint Ignatius, *The Autobiography of St. Ignatius Loyola with Related Documents*, trans. Joseph F. O'Callaghan, ed. John C. Olin (New York: Fordham University Press, 1992), chap. 1.

10. See John C. Olin, "The Idea of Pilgrimage in the Experience of Ignatius Loyola," *Church History* 48, no. 4 (December 1979): 387–97.

From the time of Ignatius as their superior general, the Jesuits have been sent on mission journeys to different parts of the world. And quite early, they entered the field of education, moving to different parts of Europe to build up schools and turning schools into shrines of knowledge and piety.

Ghazali's journey, on the other hand, got its start from the world of knowledge and learning in an academic setting. Ghazali's disillusion with mere knowledge and prestige led to a personal quest for meaning in spiritual Islam, or Sufism, which helped him acquire freedom or detachment from the snare of worldly prestige and status. His period of crisis and seclusion, which was quite long—more than ten years, from 1095 to 1106—was also the period of his greatest intellectual creativity, in which he produced, among other things, his magnum opus, *Ihya' 'ulum al-din* (*The Revival of Religious Sciences*).

When Ghazali started to embark upon this long journey of inner and outer pilgrimage in 1095, he had been teaching at the Nizamiyya Madrasa in Baghdad for a few years. Since his youth, Ghazali had been driven by a search for truth, but intense ambition also played a role. It is this conception of truth as well as his ambition that were transformed by his long pilgrimage. In Ghazali's words, the urgency of pilgrimage is described thus: "To the road! To the road! Only a little life is left and you stand on the verge of a great voyage and all your knowledge and your deeds are nothing but sham and pretense!"[11] It is interesting that Ghazali's ailment might be related to melancholia, to which scholars and academics were believed to be especially prone.[12] Furthermore, according to Eric Ormsby, "Ghazali was suffering from sheer mental and

---

11. Ghazali, *Munqidh min al-Dhalal*, 91–92, quoted in Eric Ormsby, *Ghazali* (Oxford: Oneworld, 2007), 93.
12. Ormsby, 88.

physical exhaustion and . . . this may have contributed to his spiritual distress."[13]

Ghazali's journey began when he headed for Damascus as his first destination, where he spent two years in seclusion, solitude, and meditation. He visited the Umayyad Mosque very often, spending so much of his time in a minaret that it is known to this day as "Ghazali's Minaret."[14] Then he went to Jerusalem and Hebron and made the hajj pilgrimage before returning to Damascus and making his way home to Tus to resume his teaching profession. At the end of the journey, Ghazali came back to the world of knowledge, but with different perspectives. Upon his return to teaching, Ghazali writes, "I know that even if I have returned to teaching, I haven't really returned. To return is to go back to what once was. Then I used to teach the knowledge by which prestige is acquired, and in both my words and my deeds I summoned men to that, that was my goal and my intention. But now I am summoning them to the knowledge by which prestige is relinquished and its low rank recognized."[15]

In this regard, it must be noted that "the move from sickness to health is analogous to the ascent from ignorance to knowledge, from doubt to certainty."[16] For Ghazali, as for many other medieval Muslim thinkers, ignorance is a spiritual ailment. He was also deeply troubled by the skepticism he experienced for a period of time. And so he was deeply grateful that God healed his intellectual and physical sickness during the crisis.[17]

In his early skepticism, Ghazali questioned the reliability of the senses, but after his deeper search during his long solitude, "the

---

13. Ormsby, 90.
14. Ormsby, 109.
15. Ghazali, *Munqidh min al-Dhalal*, 49–50, quoted in Ormsby, *Ghazali*, 140.
16. Ormsby, 91.
17. Ormsby, 91.

senses themselves, mysteriously, transfigured, proved to be the touchstones of truth. Taste, the least communicable of the senses, offered the final certainty, serving as a metaphor for the ultimate mystical experience."[18] Here the power of intellect was surpassed. Ghazali strongly believed that "it is not the philosophers, but the prophets who are the true 'doctors who treat the illnesses of hearts,' for they have been given insight into a further dimension of reality 'beyond the intellect.'"[19]

So what should we learn from Ignatius and Ghazali in our exploration of the relationship among pilgrimage, pedagogy, and knowledge? For those of us whose professions deal with knowledge and teaching, both as students and as teachers, these two masters show how the practice of pilgrimage can serve as a unique and rich means to form our personal identity and at the same time engage with the world of knowledge and teaching on a deeper level. In a way, Ignatius and Ghazali continued to be students throughout their lives. Their pilgrimage was a sign of the need for lifelong learning. They needed to grow spiritually. To sustain his profession as a teacher and man of knowledge, Ghazali needed a period of solitude that led to a personal transformation and a transfigured profession of teaching. And for Ignatius, he needed a long journey of conversion to better serve God by engaging the world in a mission of transformation through the Society of Jesus.

Contemporary Practices

Christian *Peregrinatio*

Arguably, the need for, and the relevance of, this kind of pilgrimage continues today. Maybe their journey is not as grand as that of Reda

---

18. Ormsby, 91.
19. Ormsby, 92.

and his aging father in *Le Grand Voyage*, but many young people today have delighted in this experience. In Indonesia, and perhaps in other countries as well, Jesuit novices (those who undergo the first two years of spiritual formation) and other seminarians would undertake this wandering pilgrimage, combining traditional pilgrimage and spiritual formation in an organized way. In the Ignatian tradition, this spiritual experiment or formation is called *peregrinatio* (peregrination), taking the model of Saint Ignatius's personal journey of conversion and spiritual formation mentioned above. In the Indonesian context, this peregrination is further contextualized not just as a practice of spiritual formation but as a rather unique means of identity formation for young Indonesian Jesuits, an identity that cannot be separated from an encounter with the role and particularities of Islam in the country.[20]

In its practice today, this *peregrinatio* is carefully designed and planned by the novice master. And it typically involves a journey of walking on foot for a period of seven to ten days, covering a distance of around 350 to 400 kilometers, starting from a certain point toward a Marian shrine or a church at its end point. The route often goes through Muslim majority areas in Java, usually through areas with local languages the novices and seminarians do not understand, thus creating a more overwhelming sense of alterity for them. During the journey, the pilgrims are required to keep the important elements of the *ordo* (daily routine) in the house of spiritual formation, such as the daily spiritual disciplines, as much as they can, with some adjustments allowed. The structure and unity of community are also kept by taking turns in serving as the superior and the "minister," who is in charge of practical matters like

---

20. Leo Agung Sardi, "La prueba de la peregrinación en el Noviciado de la Compañía de Jesús: Su actualidad para la formación en Indonesia" (PhD diss., Comillas Pontifical University, Madrid, 2016), 497.

looking for accommodations and food. Apart from the physical toll that walking on foot might inflict, the hardest part of the whole journey has to do with the fact that the novices or seminarians have no provisions at all during the entire journey, apart from a small amount of money for emergency use (or a return ticket to the novitiate or seminary). Basically, they have to beg for food and shelter.

Participants' reflections over the years clearly show that *peregrinatio* is a memorable experience, even a once-in-a-lifetime opportunity for growth. It helps inculcate in concrete ways certain spiritual virtues, such as total surrender, trust in the providential care of God, patience and perseverance, self-denial (*abnegatio sui*), humility, detachment and inner freedom, and so forth. Apart from this spiritual formation, it also plays a role in the formation of their identity and their apostolic spirit.[21]

One of the most formative dimensions of this *peregrinatio* is the experience of otherness, especially dealing with Islam and Muslims. Most of the seminarians and novices start the *peregrinatio* with a real sense of distance from and unfamiliarity with Islam and Muslims even though most of them live in Muslim majority areas with Muslim neighbors. Although they have encountered Muslims on different occasions, this does not necessarily mean that they have obtained enough closeness with Muslims to have an understanding of Islam. Against this background, the *peregrinatio* presents itself as an eye-opening experience, where these novices and seminarians can taste a sense of brotherhood with Muslims due to much more personal encounters with them. In general, the encounters are rich and dynamic, involving hard conversations around religious topics that often occur in the atmosphere of identity politics along religious lines in contemporary Indonesia. To be sure, they experience

---

21. Sardi, *Compañía de Jesús*, 420–23; B. Christian Yudo, *Peregrinasi: Eksperimen dan Cara Hidup Yesuit* (Girisonta: St. Stanislaus Novitate, 2012), 27, 30, 41, 45, 63.

occasions of rejection and suspicion, but overall, they learn valuable lessons. For example, they realize that Muslim society, like its Christian counterpart, is far from being monolithic, an awareness that defies easy stereotyping. They come to realize the humanity of Muslims face-to-face.[22] In this regard, the pilgrimage journey seems to have a special power to open their inner receptiveness and capacity for deeper communication. During the moment of pilgrimage, they are more easily touched by the kindness of others, especially Muslims. This is because they have had to beg for food and shelter; thus they have depended on Muslims to a large degree, and they have had close encounters with them. In this context, wandering pilgrimage opens more meaningful chances for moments of true kindness.

Muslim Practices: Being a *Musafir*

Indonesian Islam is also enriched by a similar practice of *peregrinatio*. Usually, the pilgrim is called a *musafir*, literally meaning "traveler" but more accurately "wandering pilgrim." The travel is meant not just for paying a visit to a sacred shrine but rather as a prolonged journey of self-reflection and spiritual formation. It might originate in a master-student relationship, where at the urging of the master, the student undergoes this spiritual journey for growth. In the context of Islamic Java, the history of this type of pilgrimage goes back to the seventeenth century. We have records of the journeys of many well-known figures who have performed this wandering pilgrimage during their formative years as youth. In fact, it was a rite of passage for young boys, especially in traditional aristocratic families of Java.[23]

---

22. Yudo, *Peregrinasi*, 53–55, 95–97, 101–3, 110–12; Sardi, *Compañía de Jesús*, 409.
23. These figures include Raden Santri, Purwa Lelono, and the great Prince Dipanegara, a famous nineteenth-century anticolonial figure. See my *Muslim and Catholic Pilgrimage*

On the major roads of Java today, we still see *musafirs*.[24] They wear distinctive attire—a big, round traditional hat; a black shirt; and a loose sarong—and they carry a simple backpack and a staff.[25] Some of the Jesuit novices and seminarians have also encountered these Muslim *musafirs* during their *peregrinatio* and had natural and amicable interactions with them.[26] These Muslim *musafirs* move from one shrine to another, typically major tombs of Muslim saints, over a longer period of time. Their motivational background and goals may vary, ranging from the need to deal with personal crises, personal devotion, the search for spiritual knowledge and growth, or a combination of these.

In the context of the local culture—namely, the Javanese culture—we must recall the special relationship between the search for knowledge and the practice of asceticism (*laku*), which has affected Islamic tradition in the area. The Javanese traditional way of true knowing always involves the role of the heart and deep affect (*rasa*), the resonance of the heart. In Javanese spirituality, *rasa* points to the deepest intuition and inner sensing. Thus, it is at once an epistemological and spiritual category.[27] In order to cultivate this inner sensing, one needs to undergo ascetic and other spiritual practices of purification of the soul, including communing with the sacred powers and the sacred figures of the past or ancestors.

In this framework of wandering pilgrimage, shrines also function as a school, where the spiritual traveler spends a longer period for their

Practices (New York: Routledge, 2014), 93–94. For Dipanegara's wandering pilgrimage, see Peter Carey, *Takdir: Riwayat Pangeran Diponegoro 1785–1855* (Jakarta: Penerbit Buku Kompas, 2014), 54–80.

24. Rijal Mumazziq Zionis, "Ziarah Melampah sebagai Jalan Dakwah," Pesantren.id, September 16, 2019, https://pesantren.id/ziarah-melampah-sebagai-jalan-dakwah-887.

25. For a description of this wandering pilgrim, see, for example, Rotibul ma'arif, "viral santri rotibul ma'arif dengan berjalan kaki keliling p jawa," uploaded on October 23, 2019, YouTube video, https://www.youtube.com/watch?v=e-v-CwZpMck.

26. Yudo, *Peregrinasi*, 109.

27. See my *Muslim and Catholic Pilgrimage Practices*, 40.

Pilgrims praying at the tomb of a local Muslim holy
man in Surabaya, Indonesia. Photo by the author.

education of the soul, which is most of the time described as purifying
the heart against the destructive lower self (*nafs*). Some pilgrims also
move from one religious school (*madrasa*) to the next. A contemporary
wandering pilgrim explains the dynamic of ascetic practices and spiritual purification this way: "We all have experienced it, namely, going
for days without provisions, surrendering ourselves to the will of God,
putting on dirty and torn clothes, all the while setting our hearts to
the remembrance of God. We walk and walk, without having a particular goal other than God; when we are hungry, we have to beg to none
other than God. Oftentimes we have to look for food in the garbage,
while sleeping in the woods, fields as well as cemeteries."[28]

---

28. Testimony of a wandering pilgrim; NN, "Spiritualnya Seorang Musafir: Perjalanan
Seorang Musafir," Kaskus.co.id, July 4, 2019, https://www.kaskus.co.id/thread/
5d1d0d156df2310ea315cf2c/spiritual-seorang-musafir/.

Personal Experience: Toward a Global Citizenship

In light of these contemporary practices, I would argue that this wandering pilgrimage can serve as a privileged moment of education for the youth, covering both spiritual and civic aspects. Within the framework of larger and deeper spiritual formation, this wandering pilgrimage cultivates civic virtues by helping forge deeper connections among citizens and building up trust. And this experience will be made much deeper and richer if it includes visiting shared pilgrimage sites or sites of the religious other.

So if I may, I would like to illustrate this dynamic of global-local citizenship by telling my own story. My first experience of *peregrinatio* was in 1994, taking the meandering four-hundred-kilometer route from the city of Bandung in West Java to the city of Purwokerto in Central Java, which I completed in nine days—a day faster than the allotted time. This route covers an area known to have a stronger Islamic identity, so in many real ways, just being in this area posed a rather serious problem of alterity for me, as I originally come from Yogyakarta, an area where Christianity forms an important and visible minority.

The first problem was that of communication, as I did not speak the local language, making begging for food and shelter a bit complicated at times. But over time, I learned how to go deeper in this art of communication. The lasting lesson for me is that by walking on foot, I had so much space for deeper communication and communion. My inner life became more focused, the eyes of my heart more attentive to details. I even got to know a local Indigenous community more closely. What is also memorable is my deeper and more personal connection with the geography and landscape of the route, which then became a meaningful place or milieu, not just an impersonal space. I had become an "emplaced self" in my wandering pilgrimage. This pilgrimage has served as a way of knowing my own culture and people in ways that are much more reflective due to the wide inner space of the encounter.[29]

I learned to get in touch with alterity or otherness on a deeper level and in fruitful ways. I remember my conversation with a Sundanese man as he was hosting me for lunch in a spirit of great hospitality. Learning that I was embarking on this wandering pilgrimage, he was talking about *yaum al-mithaq*, the day of covenant between each soul and its creator, God. At that moment, I did not know this term yet (as I would learn it much later during my doctoral studies). But I remember the crucial point: the soul was with God, and then the soul was sent to the world after making a covenant of fidelity with God. So human life is a pilgrimage of the soul back to God, with the perennial duty of remembering God. This was my first encounter with a Sufi Muslim.[30]

I did not really expect that this *peregrinatio* would serve as a distant formative experience for my own pilgrimage and studies in the Middle East in 2008–9 as part of my PhD program in comparative theology at Boston College. During my stay in Damascus, Syria, almost every weekend I would perform some sort of pilgrimage journey, mostly by public transport, but it involved a lot of walking as well. By this time, I had acquired the art of dealing with otherness. In a way, I always look forward to this moment of otherness—living in a foreign country, meeting with strangers, communicating in strange languages. I would take journeys to ancient ruins (churches, cemeteries, shrines, mosques, etc.) in remote areas, a risky journey

---

29. The famous Javanese text *Serat Centhini* (nineteenth century) imagines the collective identity of "Java" in terms of journeying to all of its sacred and potent places of all kinds while being attentive to various local customs, natural wonders, and so forth. In this text, this journeying also corresponds to the various stages in the personal growth of the human person; see also my *Muslim and Catholic Pilgrimage Practices*, 51–52.
30. My story can also be found in Yudo, *Peregrinasi*, 71–74.

for a foreigner in a country like Syria. Inside Damascus, I developed a habit of praying at places of otherness, such as the area around the tomb of Saladin, the great Muslim leader of the Crusade and the archenemy of Christian crusaders. Oftentimes I paid a visit to the Umayyad Mosque and tried to imbibe the spiritual energy of Ghazali, who spent so much time there. This deeper connection was forged in everyday life as well. Here I learned the truth of Ghazali's words when he discusses love in his magnum opus *Ihya' 'ulum al-din* (*The Revival of Religious Sciences*): "Many are the acts of God, but let us search out the least, the lowest, and the tiniest of them and contemplate their wonders."[31] What Ghazali means includes the countless number of simple marvels of the natural world and the small details of our daily lives and interactions. Through this deeper spiritual sensing, I was able to appropriate the social and natural landscape of Syria.

For most pilgrims, the practice of pilgrimage is a personal habitus that spans their lifetime, where a particular pilgrimage is part of a chain, connected to the ones before and leading to another. As I have shown, my earliest *peregrinatio* prepared me for my pilgrimage in the Middle East, and this extended pilgrimage made me much more spiritually and humanly attuned for my next pilgrimages in Europe, where I became much more attentive to otherness, especially the presence of the religious other and the painful dynamics of the encounter between Christianity and Islam. So when I returned home to do research on Islamic and Catholic pilgrimage in Java, my identity as a pilgrim had been deeply transformed and transfigured. I even enjoyed the "back-and-forth pilgrimage," in which every time I completed a visit to a Muslim shrine, I would immediately come home to a Catholic shrine in the same area in

---

31. Ghazali, *Ihya'*, 4:335–36, quoted in Ormsby, *Ghazali*, 111.

order to integrate what I had experienced at the shrine of the other into the context of my own religious tradition. This process is greatly helped by the new comparative theological method that enables me to enrich my theology and spiritual life through a deeper encounter with other religious traditions.[32]

Moving Forward

Wandering pilgrimage is a formative experience that today's youth and students can benefit from. And I believe that this can even be an attractive formation program for them. From my limited experience, this kind of pilgrimage will be fruitful with intensive preparation, especially mental and spiritual. The participants need to really know what to expect from this pilgrimage. Furthermore, stronger connection with the sacred history of the routes and their local communities will also help, for the landscape and route are not just a flat and empty space but rather a meaningful and unique place of spiritual presence and significance. Real and more personal interaction with the local peoples can be crucial for the whole learning experience. More spontaneous interaction may be better than the preplanned, but we can always improvise. Creative combinations with tourism, especially cultural and eco-tourism, can also be done and might enhance the learning experience, especially for students in general (not religious seminarians or novices). So apart from philosophical, spiritual, and theological texts, good preparation might include some traditional or classical texts on pilgrimage

---

32. See my essay "Back and Forth Riting: The Dynamics of Muslim-Christian Encounter in Shrine Rituals," in *Ritual Participation and Interreligious Dialogue: Boundaries, Transgressions and Innovations*, ed. Marianne Moyaert and Joris Geldof (London: Bloomsbury, 2015), 109–21.

journeys by certain figures as well as more modern travelogues and narratives/stories of pilgrimage journeys.

Questions for Reflection

1. Pilgrimage often involves a sense of being a stranger as well as dramatic encounters with otherness or alterity. What forms of otherness have you experienced, and what have you drawn from this experience for your own formation and that of others?

2. Pilgrimage traditions continue to develop by creating new routes and putting them in connection with the older ones. Old destinations can also be reinvented and revitalized too. In your experience, how creative are you and your group or communities in this ongoing dynamic of doing pilgrimage?

3. Encounters and connections with the local population can enrich a pilgrimage experience in many ways. How has this experience enriched you, or are you open to try to have this space of encounter in your next pilgrimage journey?

4. The search for knowledge has often been central to pilgrimage experiences for many influential persons in history. How do you relate to this notion? Does your life of study, or professional life as a teacher, involve this search for knowledge in the framework of a pilgrimage journey?

Select Annotated Bibliography

Albera, Dionigi, and John Eade, eds. *New Pathways in Pilgrimage Studies.* New York: Routledge, 2017.

    Building on earlier work by moving away from Eurasia and focusing on different areas of the world where non-Christian pilgrimages abound, this book expands the theoretical, disciplinary, and geographical perspectives of Anglophone pilgrimage studies. It covers diverse practices of pilgrimage (North Africa, South Asia, Southeast Asia, the Pacific, and Latin America) where Christian pilgrimages intersect with different traditions.

Badone, Ellen, and Sharon R. Roseman, eds. *Intersecting Journeys: The Anthropology of Pilgrimage and Tourism.* Urbana: University of Illinois Press, 2004.

    This collection of essays offers an interdisciplinary outlook on the rich and complex intersections between pilgrimage and tourism, such as conflicts over resources and meanings of the sites, the communal sense that the practices engender, and so forth. These studies shed light on postmodern debates about movement and centers, global flows, social identities, and the negotiation of meanings.

Eade, John, and Michael J. Sallnow, eds. *Contesting the Sacred: The Anthropology of Christian Pilgrimage.* Urbana: University of Illinois Press, 2000.

    Based on a number of case studies from Europe, the Holy Land, Sri Lanka and Peru, this work highlights the power of pilgrimage as a space for accommodating various, often competing, meanings and practices, both among pilgrims and between shrine custodians and devotees. This book also provides valuable insights into the process of exchange between pilgrims and the divine and the impact of globalization and tourism on pilgrimage, among others, by drawing ideas from new theoretical frameworks.

Frey, Nancy Louise. *Pilgrim Stories: On and off the Road to Santiago*. Berkeley: University of California Press, 1998.

Based on intensive fieldwork, this work is an important anthropological study on the dynamics of pilgrimage along the modern Way of St. James done by a diverse mix of largely well-educated, urban, middle-class participants who chose physically taxing journeys in order to experience nature, enjoy cultural and historical patrimony, renew faith, or cope with personal problems. This study shows that the Camino's physical and mental journey offers them a more intimate sense of community, greater personal knowledge, and meaningful connections to the past and to nature. And the transformation of life brought about by this pilgrimage often continues after they return home.

Margry, Peter Jan, ed. *Shrines and Pilgrimage in the Modern World: New Itineraries into the Sacred*. Amsterdam: Amsterdam University Press, 2008.

This book offers fresh insights into the practices of modern pilgrimage, which appear to be secular but also are deeply intertwined with human uncertainties and hopes in our complex world. Critiquing the inadequacy of the notion of the secular and the sacred, this work employs new ethnographical and theoretical approaches on the interesting subject of modern pilgrimage.

Chapter 8

The Steepness of the Pilgrim Path

Ascetic Lessons from Student-Pilgrims in Japan

John A. Shultz
Kansai Gaidai University

As students from my course titled Pilgrimage: Journeys in Search of Meaning ascend the Kirarazaka Trail on Mount Hiei, a recursive connection is realized between themselves and the many famous and common Japanese pilgrims who have climbed before them. The uniquely famed holy mountain just north of Kyoto is a site of faithful devotion, but it is also a place where living Buddhas are made through ascetic pilgrimage efforts that are arguably the most severe on the planet. In addition to performing a life-threatening fast from food and water for seven days, the *Hiei Kaihōgyōja*, or "marathon monks" of Mount Hiei, spend seven years engaging in intervals of walking between holy sites in and around the mountain. They will traverse more than forty thousand kilometers, a distance equivalent to the circumference of the earth. By the end of the practice, the monks are moving the length of two marathons a day continuously for one hundred days. This mountain is also a place of "dark pilgrimage": it is the site of a massacre of as many as twenty thousand Buddhist monks and their supporters by the warlord Oda

Nobunaga in 1571 CE. But in the context of our eight-hundred-meter ascent of the mountain, the student-pilgrims (both international and native Japanese) find their attention almost entirely focused on the next steep footstep and the heaving in their chests. Some ponder whether they have made a serious error by agreeing to the climb, even after forewarnings that the university's most physically demanding field trip requires negotiating the equivalent of 230 flights of steps. Nonetheless, they are all volunteers on this one-day pilgrimage climb. Furthermore, the students have elected not to mollify the difficulties by taking one of two popular cable cars up the flanks of the mountain. Quite simply, they have embraced the simple notion that difficulty and profundity of meaning are inseparably linked in the pilgrimage environment.

Scholars, students, and practitioners of pilgrimage should fundamentally understand that the basic character of a sacred journey is shaped in a primary way by relative austerity.

In our initial classroom discussions of sacred travel, students are generally quite adamant that any notion of pilgrimage must include challenge and self-deprivation. This modest but critical assertion is largely substantiated when we consider specific Japanese examples of pilgrimage throughout the course, including the so-called walking austerities of Mount Hiei itself and the ascetic orientations of Japan's most famous pilgrimage, the Shikoku *henro*. In the context of their own exploratory projects—around which the course is centered—many young scholars choose to either replicate the challenges of those who came before or creatively design their own new trials that they hope will unlock the deep meaning of travel.

I have argued elsewhere that pilgrimage studies should treat the basic meaning of pilgrimage as an independent variable that changes with respect to an entire range of dependent variables, such as time spent pilgrimaging, the social nature of the travel, and how much free choice individuals have with regard to their journeys.[1] At the heart of this course, students are challenged to fundamentally probe specific meanings of "pilgrimage": a task that can veer toward either the social scientific or the theological/dharmalogical. They are required to engage in a research and exploratory project that constitutes the bulk of their grade. For this project, students are encouraged to design and execute their own journeys of meaning. While their choices must be adequately justified, they are allowed significant latitude in their personal explorations of pilgrimage.

Ascetic Meanings and Variability

Before we delve deeper, I must clarify what we mean by asceticism. Geoffrey Harpham reflects deeply on the topic, drawing from European Christian contexts. He explains that asceticism loosely "refers to any act of self-denial undertaken as a strategy of empowerment or gratification."[2] More significantly, he boldly argues that a general human appeal to ethics is itself "inescapably ascetical" and that asceticism is *the* universal driver of culture.[3] Despite its centrality to civilization and humanity, Harpham posits that asceticism is not so much an idea as an ambivalent drive, which seems to both condemn culture and endorse it,[4] to deny the human body and to dignify it.[5] Agreeing with sentiments from William James,

---

1. John A. Shultz, "Pilgrimaging through Time: The Theoretical Implications of Continuing Journeys on the Shikoku Henro," *International Journal of Religious Tourism and Pilgrimage* 8, no. 1 (2020): 51–59.
2. Geoffrey Galt Harpham, *The Ascetic Imperative in Culture and Criticism*, 2nd ed. (Chicago: University of Chicago Press, 1992), xiii.
3. Harpham, xi.
4. Harpham, xiii.
5. Harpham, xiv.

he maintains that asceticism is not limited to religious phenomena and can be found "in wholly secular practices and institutions."[6]

My own research concerning Japanese sacred journeys, especially the Shikoku *henro*, seems to reinforce Harpham's assertions. The Shikoku *henro* is a 1,400-kilometer pilgrimage circuit that links eighty-eight holy places. The *henro* has gradually risen in prominence over the last 350 years to become the country's definitive spiritual journey. The faithful trace its origins all the way back to the time of Kūkai (774–835 CE), the man who brought Shingon esoteric Buddhism to Japan from China. However, the *henro* has been popularized in its current form only since the Edo period (1603–1867 CE), the dawn of the early modern era. Contemporary pilgrims circumnavigate the island and the eighty-eight temples by various means: through structured and ritually formal bus tours, their own personal vehicles, public transportation, bicycling, walking, or a combination of any number of modes. Significantly, the story of the *henro* is essentially the story of how the paths and locations of wandering itinerants grew into a popular, systematized form of religious expression that still maintains a rich discourse of asceticism.

The Shikoku *henro* shows that pilgrimages can derive popularity by providing a continuum of challenges that can accommodate a fantastic range of preferences regarding austerities. At one extreme, I have seen a single steep set of stairs within a temple described as an "ascetic practice" by an elderly and slightly infirm pilgrim traveling by car. At another extreme, my work with Ian Reader, a foremost scholar of Japanese religion and pilgrimage studies, has profiled permanent itinerants, who have walked hundreds of thousands of kilometers in continual circumambulation of the *henro*, sleeping

---

6. Harpham, xiii.

roughshod outdoors, living off of alms, and having their skin turn to a sort of leather from constant exposure to the elements.[7]

A case study of written personal accounts I conducted with respect to contemporary Japanese Buddhist priests on the *henro* shows a universal vision of the experience as an ascetic practice.[8] However, when we drill down to consider how they describe asceticism with regard to their respective pilgrimages, we find it to be a very relative concept and something that often manifests itself more in things to do, or not to do, in the context of their travel, such as making a personal rule to solicit alms daily or to forgo alcohol or motorized transportation. We will see that students in the pilgrimage course often similarly try to seek an ideal balance in creating a journey that has meaning wrought from challenge but is still manageable.

The Mountains That Make Buddhas

Kōbō Daishi is the saintly name for the Buddhist priest Kūkai (774–835 CE), the founder of Shingon esoteric Buddhism in Japan. He has come to embody the ultimate pilgrim for this island nation. The Daishi—as he is affectionately known—is universally understood to be both a historically great Japanese person and something akin to an archetype of an enlightened individual. As with the Tendai Buddhist tradition of the *Kaihōgyōja* mentioned, the Daishi exemplifies how ascetic travels can make one a Buddha in a single lifetime. He is the central figure for the Shikoku *henro* as well as hundreds of smaller pilgrimages that copy the structure

---

7. Ian Reader and John Shultz, *Pilgrims until We Die: Unending Pilgrimage in Shikoku* (Oxford: Oxford University Press, 2021).
8. John A. Shultz, "The Way to Gyō: Priestly Asceticism on the Shikoku Henro," *Japanese Journal of Religious Studies* 43, no. 2 (2016): 275–305.

of this eighty-eight-place institution. Likewise, the Daishi is historically associated with two other significant mountain pilgrimage locations: Mount Inari in Kyoto, the holiest of holies for the Indigenous Inari deity, and Mount Kōya in Wakayama prefecture, the location of Kūkai's head monastery.

As seen with ascetics around the world, mountains are natural monasteries for edifying transformation. Because nearly every significant peak in the country—from Mount Fuji on down—has religious significance, climbing is arguably the most fundamental form of ascetic practice in Japan. For example, the Japanese term *gyōba*, the most basic term for ascetic practice locations, generally indicates steep rock outcrops, which are often equipped with in situ chains and other climbing aids.

Steep and wild locations around the island of Shikoku that instinctively drew individual ascetics would subsequently become sacred locations of the *henro*. The earliest legends of the boy who would become Kūkai/Kōbō Daishi describe him scaling a precarious cliff on a mountain above his home at Zentsuji in Sanuki Province. His dramatic rock climb ends with a leap of faith to show his resolve for his spiritual calling, after which he is saved by an angel sent by Shakyamuni Buddha. The location for this story is the innermost sanctuary of Temple 73, Shusshakaji. Likewise, Kūkai's own writings record his ascetic trials on the sheer and exposed peaks of Shikoku: climbing dangerous rock ridges, facing incapacitating snow, running out of food, and enduring exposed bivouacs. He specifically records ascending Mount Ishizuchi, a famous holy site for mountain austerities, which has become a sort of nexus encompassing numerous numbered locations for the *henro* (Temples 44, 45, and 61–64).[9] The enlightened spiritual climax of the priest's asceticism on the island is

---

9. See Yoshito S. Hakeda, *Kukai: Major Works*, reprint ed. (New York: Columbia University Press, 1972), 22.

said to have taken place in a cave next to the Pacific Ocean in Tosa Province, where his mind was freed from all worldly desires.

Very importantly for sacred culture in Japan, the Daishi is viewed as an eternal ascetic and pilgrim. There are two contexts where he enjoys a perpetual existence in the minds of the faithful: in a state of eternal meditation on Mount Kōya and as a constant shape-shifting pilgrim on the Shikoku *henro*. On Mount Kōya he is described as passing into *nyujo*, literally "entering the mountain for austerities" but implying a state of *samadhi*, a deep state of meditative concentration. Even today, attendant monks are believed to enter Kōbō Daishi's mausoleum to provide him with food and to groom him. With respect to the Shikoku *henro*, tradition also maintains that any pilgrim one encounters could be the Daishi himself. As such, local people on the island are especially careful to show consideration to any wandering seeker they might encounter. Thus, the Daishi is a model of the eternal pilgrim, a living Buddha ever present on the pilgrim trails of the island.

The Scholar-Pilgrim, Language Training, and Study Abroad

Generally speaking, education has strong associations with asceticism in Japanese culture. From the time of Kūkai to the early modern period, Buddhist institutions in Japan were the primary means of learning, giving education in the country a decidedly austere character. Even today, middle school and high school students are required to clean the school lavatories, a throwback to humbling and edifying monastic chores deemed integral to personal development. With the notion that learning requires a degree of self-mortification, air conditioning and heating are often used quite sparingly in Japanese schools, even in university classrooms.

A statue of Kōbō Daishi at the gate of Temple 24, Hotsumisakiji, of the Shikoku *henro*. Image by author and used with permission.

The striking counterpart to the Daishi's wilderness austerities is his educational training in cities, enabling him to become an international conduit for Buddhist teachings. Tales of his early years studying a Confucian curriculum in Japan's capital are a testament to his vigorous mind, even though he lacked material advantages, such as funds for lamp oil that allowed students to study after dark. Indeed, his status as the premier esoteric Buddhist of his era owes as much to his long hours of scholarly training as to his wilderness exploits. Indeed, his epic international voyage to China in search of truth is motivated by his scholarly training.

Pilgrimages in Asia have often centered on the acquisition of religious texts or quests to discover a text's true meaning, reinforcing the need for worthy pilgrims to devote significant time to language study. Indeed, the epic journey of the monk Xuanzang (602–64 CE) from Chang'an, the ancient capital of China, along the China Silk Road to India to seek Mahayana Buddhist texts becomes an archetype for pilgrimage. As a result of Wu Cheng-en's famous *Journey to the West*, which creates a satirical allegory loosely connected to the historical quest, this pilgrimage story evolves into one of the most famous narratives in Asia. Kūkai would naturally have a deep connection to the pilgrimage of Xuanzang, as he trained and studied esoteric Buddhism at Seiryuji Temple in Chang'an, where the exploits of the Chinese monk are dramatically commemorated at the famous Giant Wild Goose Pagoda. Indeed, there is continuity between the two great pilgrims with respect to Chang'an, as contemporary Japanese *henro* pilgrims sometimes trek to Seiryuji, and this temple is affectionately termed holy place zero of the eighty-eight-place Shikoku pilgrimage. As such, the ancient capital of China links Buddhist India to Japan and also China's most famous spiritual journey to Japan's definitive pilgrimage.

Kūkai's own epic journey to China is generally presented as a quest for the true meaning of the Dainichi Sutra, a text that no contemporary Japanese scholar could adequately explain to him. As such, his intensive studies of classical Chinese and Sanskrit become central to his international pilgrimage. Kūkai's linguistic skills were so renowned that he is given legendary credit for creating *hiragana*, an essential syllabary that allows the Japanese to pronounce Chinese ideograms. Furthermore, another famous tale relates how Kūkai and his shipmates were denied entry permits to disembark from their ship in China until the priest made a written appeal in impeccable Chinese that deeply impressed a local magistrate with both its form and its sincerity.

Kūkai, his contemporary Saichō, and numerous subsequent Japanese monks who went to China would return to alter the course of Japanese religious history and to profoundly shape discourse regarding sacred travel. For example, the Tendai Buddhist monk Ennin would write extensively about his own epic journey to China and, in doing so, would coin the term *junrei*, the most general expression for pilgrimage in Japan that roughly translates to "going around and worshipping." Quite importantly, these pilgrims would establish a conflation between austere pilgrimage and that which we would now commonly call "study abroad."

The Pilgrimage Course Project: Goals, Mentoring, and Formats

Students in the pilgrimage course that I have regularly taught for almost twelve years become personally familiar with the archetypical ascetic examples of Japanese pilgrims and also the study-abroad aspects associated with them. Since these young seekers are either preparing for study abroad or in the act of it, they are already predisposed to the simple notion that the pains of international travel and learning are a source of deep meaning and significant life changes. As such, their experiential and/or scholarly pilgrimage quests can sometimes be viewed as an extension of a journey already underway or as a pilgrimage within a pilgrimage. Recognizing this basic condition, I have endeavored to use the course and its central project to further inspire and cultivate the minds of student-pilgrims. To that end, I would like to outline some points of consideration.

Numerous commendable examples in this volume seek to rally students around a single, shared pilgrimage experience. However, my purpose is to empower them to take up divergent paths suited to their own predispositions. In some cases, these individually chosen journeys may harken in spirit to the innovative quests of foundational pilgrims rather than the subsequent pilgrimages that follow in such footsteps. As a pedagogical goal, I hope that these experiences might remain impactful in the students' minds ten years out from the course, but an ultimate aim would be to create an experience of a lifetime. In order to accommodate this simple goal and the significant range of divergent pilgrim paths, the educator must (1) have a thorough working knowledge of the myriad manifestations of meaningful travel and (2) be willing to spend significant amounts of time with students one-on-one to cultivate their ideal projects.

My first mistake early on in teaching this course was to adhere too rigidly to a required written paper format for the project, consisting of x number of words, x number of academic sources, and so on, instead of allowing for more creative expressions of the meaning found in travel. Academic papers offer inspiration to only a select minority of students. Likewise, Japanese pilgrims have always commemorated their journeys with the production of art:

Kūkai/Kōbō Daishi is believed to have carved sacred Buddhist images that became the central focus of holy sites, while Matsuo Bashō, following in the literary footsteps of his itinerant poet-heroes, used religious wandering as his ultimate artistic muse. Numerous other pilgrims have created drawings, music, photo collections, or creative writings to convey the impact of sacred journeys. Secondarily, art itself has increasingly become an organizing series of destinations for student pilgrimages, as locations in Japan, such as the island of Naoshima in Kagawa Prefecture, have created multisite art pilgrimages mirroring the structures of traditional sacred journeys. Thus, realizing my restrictive error, I opened the project up first to the use of film and later to the inclusion of original art of various descriptions. In short, art has significantly increased the profundity of this project.

Film has become an especially popular means of expression for student-pilgrim projects, accounting for roughly half of submissions in recent years. User-friendly hardware and software with the ability to produce professional-level films are easily and cheaply available. I have employed film-making projects in all of my courses for more than ten years, resulting in over seven hundred student film submissions. An educator should have a firm grasp of the basic film-making process and its related tools, especially with regard to editing, in order to properly evaluate and mentor such projects.

Practically speaking, I have developed several conventions for film projects. Rather than contend with any number of video file types, it is best to have the students upload their films to either cloud-based resources like Google Drive or Dropbox or standard video-sharing websites like YouTube or Vimeo. Students then submit the URLs for the projects through the university's online platform or Google Forms. While I am willing to allow significant latitude—even experimentation—in the style and orientation of the film (e.g., vlog, animation, documentary style, third person, gonzo journalism, and so forth), students are forbidden from simply recording a traditional oral presentation. For a pilgrimage project worth 60 percent of the final grade in the seminar, a minimum length requirement of ten minutes has proven to be generally optimal.

Student Visions of Ascetic Journeys

While ascetic orientations tend to dominate student-defined understandings of pilgrimage, I should note that a number of excellent projects throughout the history of the course have had little or no appeal to austerity. For example, a high-quality recent effort considered the myriad flowers of famous holy sites in the Kansai region. Numerous works have related to popular fandom with connections to manga, anime, or gaming. Several well-executed projects on Christian pilgrimage in the greater Nagasaki region of Japan have been far more faith oriented and commemorative in scope. However, in this final section, I would like to profile three specific student visions of ascetic travel that are viewed as personally transformative and therefore carry a certain gravity in these pilgrims' lives.[10]

Anna Duong-Topp was working toward a double major in religious studies and Japanese at Gustavus Adolphus College when she came to study with us at Kansai Gaidai University. As a devoted follower of Zen Buddhism, she chose to embark on a scholarly and physical journey of interreligious dialogue with the Shingon esoteric Buddhist tradition. Her pursuit culminated in a pilgrimage to Mount Kōya, the holiest of holies for the religion and—as we have

---

10. All three students kindly provided me with written consent in July 2021 to share the content of their projects in this chapter.

seen—the location where Kōbō Daishi is said to be living in a state of eternal *samadhi*. While reinforcing her commitment to her own tradition, Anna immersed herself in a study of Shingon doctrine. In her paper, she carefully considers the esoteric tradition with respect to discrimination and patriarchy, musing on the premodern history of the prohibition of women entering the mountain's precincts. She understood well that this sacred location is known as a place for austere training with the potential to become "a Buddha in this very body," or *sokushin jobutsu* in Japanese. Thus, Anna chose to engage the aesthetic and ascetic by staying in temple lodging, composing reflective haiku, copying Buddhist holy texts, and practicing *ajikan*, a focused esoteric style of meditation on the Sanskrit character *A*, which the tradition maintains is the fastest means to enlightenment. Anna describes her experiences with wonderful detail and penetrating rational self-reflection. In her carefully selected words, you can feel the genuine sense of existential struggle as she tries to contextualize the lessons of the dramatic landscape and the potently challenging practices. She ultimately concludes her reflection by dubbing her journey a "cathartic pilgrimage."

At first consideration, the "*sake* pilgrimage" of Ludvig Lormark Friis, a Japanese language major from the University in Gothenburg in Sweden, sounds like a sort of spring break bacchanal flowing freely with the alcohol brewed from rice. However, in truth, this effort was arguably the most austere journey ever undertaken by one of our students. Japanese *sake* has deep religious significance for Shinto; as one priest succinctly put it to me, "The *kami* love *sake*." This centrality can be seen by its ritual inclusion in everything from weddings to the final send-off of kamikaze pilots. Luddie, as he is affectionately known, combined his deep interest in *sake* with his passion for hiking. He chose to walk from the university in Hirakata in Osaka Prefecture to the three most famous Shinto shrines associated with the sacred beverage, two located in Kyoto and one in Nara. I should note that this is not an established pilgrimage circuit, and Luddie may well have been the first person to purposely link these sites through a walking pilgrimage. Along the way, he also made stops in Kyoto at the famous *sake* brewing district of Fushimi and to take in the famous Philosopher's Path. This intrepid 114.67-kilometer walk was done over the course of two days on a weekend during the height of the cherry blossoms, giving his professional-looking HD film an almost otherworldly quality. The journey concludes well into the night with his weary arrival at Ōmiwa Shrine, which is understood to be the oldest Shinto shrine in Japan. While his organizing theme is sacred *sake*, his journey is an exposé of the simple act of walking as an austere act of self-discovery.

"Why don't I do the things I know will make me happy?" Elena Hoh, a fibers and material practices major from Concordia University in Montreal, pondered this simple question in the context of her decision to undergo a personalized version of a traditional pilgrimage practice on Mount Inari in Fushimi, Kyoto. This mountain is the location of arguably the most famous and visually striking Shinto shrine in all of Japan, Fushimi Inari Taisha, which is renowned for its tens of thousands of wood and stone *torii* gates. The Inari kami is Japan's most popular Indigenous deity and is associated with prayers for good harvest, success in business, and career advancement. The fox is understood to be the messenger of the Inari kami, and thousands of fox images dot the mountainside. The *shichi-do mairi* was a grueling ascetic practice popular among noblewomen in the Heian period (794–1185 CE). The pilgrimage has the practitioner climb up the flanks of Mount Inari (233 m) seven times through the grounds of the Fushimi Inari Taisha shrine. Elena's pilgrimage, which she purposely designates as "practice," was a simple variation on this old tradition: climb the holy mountain eight times and after each climb, channel your inspired state of mind by drawing an image in a Japanese pilgrim stamp book, or *shuincho*. She explains simply that through this disciplined ascetic practice, she hopes to overcome a tendency to slide into "nongenerative activities" (e.g., eating lying down, watching TV, wasting an entire day) that she knows do not bring her happiness and that cause her to descend toward a sort of paralysis in life. Elena's experiences were chronicled in an exquisite film, employing rich audio and artistic camera angles of trees, stones, cherry blossoms, *torii* gates, fox images, and mesmerizing video clips of her drawing pilgrimage-inspired pictures. The goal of this austerity was to achieve the powerful original childlike state of existence, where actions flow naturally and a state of nonduality exists between the mind and body. Remarkably, the film itself draws the viewer into the sort of trance-like or meditative state, proving the ultimate aim of her carefully designed pilgrimage practice.

Conclusion

As is so often the case, our seemingly rough attempts to inspire students as educators conversely end up showing us some unexpected profundity. The physical and allegorical struggles of student-pilgrims in Japan to ascend their self-chosen holy mountain have fundamentally changed the way I methodologically, analytically, and theoretically consider the phenomena of sacred travel. Specifically, in my attempts to aid them on their respective journeys, students like Anna, Luddie, and Elena have shown me the true interpretive value of asceticism as a key variable in pilgrimage studies. Their projects—respectively, academic, corporeal, and artistic—are representative of dozens of valiant efforts by young seekers in the course striving to comprehend the potent meaning of travel. I believe these examples of archetypical Japanese pilgrims encourage students studying in Japan to engage with the remarkable potential present when pilgrimage is thoughtfully incorporated into a university curriculum.

Questions for Reflection

1. Pilgrimage can center both on natural locations and on human-made structures. Can you offer specific examples of more nature-oriented or more shrine-oriented pilgrimages? Do you find yourself attracted more to one style or another?

2. If you were to design your own journey of self-transformation, would you include purposeful acts of self-denial and/or structured physical challenges? On your quest, what things might you prohibit and what things might you require?

3. In Western religious contexts, we often think of pilgrimage as a chance to commune with the divine. However, in Asian settings, we can sometimes understand sacred journeys as a means for one to become a Buddha. Can both types of journeys legitimately be considered the same phenomenon?

4. Anna's trip to Mount Kōya is an example of pilgrimage as interreligious dialogue. Can you think of other famous examples in contexts outside of Japan? How committed must a person be to one's faith before taking up the yoke of pilgrimage?

Select Annotated Bibliography

Harpham, Geoffrey Galt. *The Ascetic Imperative in Culture and Criticism*. 2nd ed. Chicago: University of Chicago Press, 1992.

This text provides a bold, thought-provoking thesis on the connection between asceticism and culture. As such, it raises critical issues for the study of sacred travel.

Reader, Ian. *Making Pilgrimages: Meaning and Practice in Shikoku*. Honolulu: University of Hawai'i Press, 2005.

This is the most thorough and complete treatment in the English language concerning one of the world's most important pilgrimages: the Shikoku *henro*. It should be required reading for any serious scholar of pilgrimage studies.

———. *Pilgrimage: A Very Short Introduction*. Illustrated edition. London: Oxford University Press, 2015.

While scholars of sacred travel tend to have either Eastern or Western orientations, this introduction provides a truly global perspective. The book is an excellent starting point for educators new to the field.

Reader, Ian, and John Shultz. *Pilgrims until We Die: Unending Pilgrimage in Shikoku*. Oxford: Oxford University Press, 2021.

This text draws from extensive contemporary fieldwork using the Shikoku *henro* as a case study to show that pilgrimage activities can become a centralizing principle for the continuing lives of practitioners. The text challenges key paradigms in the field.

Ryotaro, Shiba. *Kukai the Universal: Scenes from His Life*. New York: ICG Muse, 2003.

This is the most famous treatment of one of Japan's most seminal religious figures. The narrative of Kūkai demonstrates how pilgrimage created a Buddhist saint.

Shultz, John A. "The Way to Gyō: Priestly Asceticism on the Shikoku Henro." *Japanese Journal of Religious Studies* 43, no. 2 (2016): 275–305.

This article takes an in-depth look at the language of pilgrimage ascetic practice in Japan. It shows that asceticism is ill suited to a strict definition.

Stavans, Ilan, and Joshua Ellison. "Reclaiming Travel." *New York Times: Opinionator* (blog), July 7, 2012. https://tinyurl.com/ttykaa38.

This is a thoughtful short argument on the role of challenge for meaningful travel. It is an ideal basis for a spirited classroom discussion.

Stevens, John. *The Marathon Monks of Mount Hiei*. Reprint ed. Brattleboro, VT: Echo Point Books and Media, 2015.

This is a popular treatment replete with numerous illustrations of what is arguably the world's most grueling pilgrimage ascetic practice. The extreme nature of the walking austerity and its do-or-die character make for great material for classroom discussions.

Yu, Anthony C., trans. *The Monkey and the Monk: An Abridgment of the Journey to the West*. 1st ed. Chicago: University of Chicago Press, 2006.

This is my recommended translation of the most famous fictional pilgrimage narrative in East Asia. *The Journey to the West* is a deeply satirical look at beastly pilgrims on the Silk Road, and the story invites natural comparisons to *The Wonderful Wizard of Oz*.

Chapter 9

Visiting Xóotoum Ngor as a Catholic

Opportunities and Challenges of Autoethnography for Pilgrimage Studies

Nougoutna Norbert Litoing, SJ
Harvard University

Over the years, I have visited various Muslim (Sufi) pilgrimage[1] sites in Senegal, both as a researcher and as a person of faith. Integrating these two dimensions of my identity is not without challenges. In some academic quarters, sound research would require that, on such visits, I bracket my identity as a person of faith for the sake of supposed scientific objectivity. Failure to do so would undoubtedly cast a dark cloud over the academic credentials of the work I do. On the other hand, in some religious circles, visiting these shrines as a person of faith would require that I set aside the critical/rational lens of my academic training as a prerequisite to experiencing the *mysterium tremendum et fascinans* (awe-inspiring and fascinating mystery) to which these shrines bear witness. In these circles, a further layer of complexity arises by virtue of the fact that as a Roman Catholic, I claim to visit Sufi shrines as a

---

1. Within the Islamic tradition, the pilgrimage practice attached to such shrines is known as *ziyara* (visit). It is different from the canonical pilgrimage to Mecca (hajj), one of Islam's five pillars, and the lesser pilgrimage (*umrah*).

believer. Doctrinal purists will undoubtedly frown upon such boundary crossing. There is consequently a real risk of finding one-self in limbo, neither here nor there, be it regarding the interfaith (Muslim-Christian) dimension of my undertaking or its academic/devotional component. At the end of the day, endeavoring to hold together the two facets of my identity entails running the risk that my undertaking and the writing that stems from it might neither satisfy the believer nor command the respect of the academic.

As such, is it possible or even desirable to seek to reconcile one's personal (inner) life and academic pursuit? This question lies at the heart of this reflection, which seeks to highlight the opportunities and challenges of autoethnography for pilgrimage studies. My visit to a shrine of the Layeniyya, a Senegalese Sufi order founded by Seydina Limamou Laye (1843–1909), serves as the pretext for this reflection. Some of the teachings of this Sufi order will undoubtedly be considered unorthodox by many Muslims. However, assessing the orthodoxy or lack thereof of Layene teachings is beyond the scope of this chapter. It merely seeks to highlight some of the lessons learned with regard to methodology while visiting a pilgrimage site associated with this community.

After a brief presentation of the Layene, I offer a similarly brief overview of autoethnography. The third part of this reflection provides an account of three stations of my visit at the shrine of Xóotoum Ngor. All along, I make the effort to connect my personal experience with broader cultural/social trends in Senegal.

The Layene of Senegal

In 1884, a Lebu fisherman named Libasse Thiaw declared that he was the *madhi*[2] and the bodily reincarnation of the Prophet

---

2. In Islam, the *mahdi*, or "rightly guided one," is an eschatological messianic figure. He is a reformer, tasked with restoring true religion and ushering in an era of justice and equity.

Muhammad.[3] He would become known to his followers as Seydina Limamou Laye (*lit.*, our master, the imam of God). The members of the ensuing order, almost exclusively from the Lebu ethnic group, refer to themselves as Layene (Wolof for "people of Allah"). Seydina Limamou Laye did not leave any writings. Rather, his core teachings are contained in a series of six sermons delivered in Wolof during his ministry and later translated into Arabic and French by Layene scholars.[4] His son and first successor, Seydina Issa Rohou Laye (*lit.*, our master, Jesus the beloved of God) is perceived by the Layene as the reincarnation of Jesus. The hagiographies of both figures are equally important sources for justifying Layene beliefs and practices. One notable aspect of Layene belief and practice has to do with the equality of believers, transcending distinctions of race, ethnicity, class, and occupational caste. At Layene gatherings, this equality is expressed in a dress code meant to render the distinction between rich and poor invisible. Social justice is viewed as a corollary of this teaching on equality.

The Layene have exhibited a fluid identity over time. The first generation described the movement as a *confrérie* (brotherhood) in order to carve out a place for the community among the larger Senegalese Sufi orders that constitute much of the religious fabric of the nation. However, younger Layene scholars reject this label, opting instead to portray their community as an Islamic reform movement stressing social justice and having an international rather than a national scope.

---

3. For a history of the origins of the Layene, see Cécile Laborde, *La Confrérie layenne et les Lébou du Sénégal: Islam et culture traditionnelle en Afrique* (Bordeaux: Presses Universitaires de Bordeaux, 1995). The primary sources related to the history of the community are made available in French on the official website of the community, http://www.layene.sn. These are mainly two series of sermons, one given by Limamou Laye and the other by his son, Issa Rohou Laye.

4. For the teachings of Seydina Limamou Laye, see Ababacar Laye Basse, *Les Enseignements de Seydina Limamou Lahi (PSL)* (Dakar: Muslim Scholars, 2003).

Seydina Limamou Laye opened his ministry with the *Appel* (call): "*Aajiibo daa-i Yaa Lahi* [respond to God's call]! The Prophet Muhammad was asleep. Now he has awoken and God has put his soul in my body. I am the Prophet of God, the *Mahdi*."[5] The Layene commemorate the *Appel* each year by undertaking a *ziyara* (pious visitation) or pilgrimage to the sites recalling important events or beliefs associated with the life of their founder. Five such sites exist on the Cap-Vert Peninsula.

The first site is a cliffside cave known as Xóotoum Ngor, in the Almadies sector of Dakar, the capital city of Senegal. The Layene believe that the spirit of the Prophet Muhammad came to reside in this cave following his death in Arabia. This spirit was reincarnated in Seydina Limamou Laye, their founder. The second site is located in Yoff (specifically Yoff-Layene). This is a multifaceted site. Not only is it the birthplace of Seydina Limamou Laye; it is equally the site of his mausoleum, the residence of the khalif (his successor), and the main headquarters of the brotherhood. The third site is located in Malika, where Limamou Laye was arrested by French colonial troops. In Layene hagiography, this arrest is associated with the founder's *hijra*.[6] The fourth site is on the island of Gorée, best known in history as having been a major slave-trading center but remembered in Layene circles for its role as the place of Limamou Laye's exile. Finally, the fifth site is Cambérène,[7] where Limamou Laye was allowed to reside after his release by the French. Cambérène is

---

5. See Ababacar Laye Basse, *Les Enseignements de Seydina Limamou Lahi (PSL)* (Dakar: Muslim Scholars, 2003), cited in Emily Riley, "'Guests of God': The Layene, an Urban Sufi Community of Dakar, Senegal," *Africa Today* 66, no. 1 (2019): 123.

6. The *hijra* in Islam refers to the migration of Muhammad and his followers from Mecca to Yathrib to establish the ideal Muslim polity. Yathrib will become Medina (from *al-madina*, Ar. "the city").

7. Lebu translation of "comme Médine" (like Medina). This is where the Layene were first able to put the teachings of the founder into practice, organizing the life of the community following these teachings.

Cliffside cave on the Atlantic Ocean. Photo by the author.

equally the site of the mausoleum of Limamou Laye's first khalif. Xóotoum Ngor, Yoff, and Cambérène are the three main pilgrimage sites visited annually during the commemoration of the *Appel.* This reflection is based on my visit (pilgrimage) to Xóotoum Ngor. Before delving into the said visit, it would be expedient to briefly outline the methodological approach adopted for the purpose of this project.

A Brief Overview of Autoethnography as a Method

Stemming from the field of anthropology, autoethnography is a qualitative research method that emerged in response to "the calls to place greater emphasis on the ways in which the ethnographer interacts with the culture being researched."[8] Heewon Chang argues that in this regard, autoethnography "shares the storytelling feature with other genres of self-narrative but transcends mere narration of self to engage in cultural analysis and interpretation."[9] In this sense, autoethnography holds autobiography and ethnography in a positive tension. This said, there are probably as many definitions of autoethnography as there are autoethnographers.

Nonetheless, C. Ellis and A. P. Bochner have insightfully highlighted the triadic model that cuts across all definitions. They argue that "autoethnographers vary in their emphasis on the research process (graphy), on culture (ethno), and on self (auto)" and that "different exemplars of autoethnography fall at different places along the continuum of these three axes."[10] Based on this triadic model,

---

8. Nicholas L. Holt, "Representation, Legitimation, and Autoethnography: An Autoethnographic Writing Story," *International Journal of Qualitative Methods* 2, no. 1 (2003): 18.

9. Heewon Chang, *Autoethnography as Method* (New York: Routledge, 2016), 43.

10. C. Ellis and A. P. Bochner, "Autoethnography, Personal Narrative, Reflexivity: Researcher as Subject," in *Handbook of Qualitative Research*, ed. N. K. Denzin and Y. S. Lincoln (London: Sage, 2000), 740.

Chang argues that "autoethnography should be ethnographic in its methodological orientation, cultural in its interpretive orientation, and autobiographical in its content orientation."[11]

Despite the waxing interest in self-narratives in anthropology, autoethnography has received some pushback. Among other critics, Philip Carl Salzman frowns upon what he views as a postmodern obsession with self-reflexivity and with ethnographer subjectivity. In his assessment, this obsession stalls the progress of anthropology.[12] Salzman's criticism reflects a call to uphold scientific objectivity in the face of a methodological trend in which the researcher's subjectivity could hold too much sway. The tension between objectivity and subjectivity has led to the emergence of different camps within autoethnography. Some scholars argue for a more analytical, theoretical, and objective approach to autoethnography,[13] while others argue for a more evocative, emotionally engaging, more subjective autoethnography.[14] A third group of scholars tries to reconcile both positions.[15]

Visit to Xóotoum Ngor

Getting Started

Going on pilgrimage to Xóotoum Ngor required some preparation. It notably took several weeks to get a reliable contact within

---

11. Chang, *Autoethnography as Method*, 48.
12. Philip Carl Salzman, "On Reflexivity," *American Anthropologist* 104, no. 3 (2002): 805–13.
13. See L. Anderson, "Analytic Autoethnography," *Journal of Contemporary Ethnography* 35, no. 4 (2006): 373–95; and P. Atkinson, "Rescuing Autoethnography," *Journal of Contemporary Ethnography* 35, no. 4 (2006): 400–404.
14. See C. S. Ellis and A. P. Bochner, "Analyzing Analytic Autoethnography," *Journal of Contemporary Ethnography* 35, no. 4 (2006): 429–49; and N. Denzin, "Analytic Autoethnography, or Déjà Vu All over Again," *Journal of Contemporary Ethnography* 35, no. 4 (2006): 419–28.
15. See J. Best, "What, We Worry? The Pleasures and Costs of Defective Memory for Qualitative Sociologists," *Journal of Contemporary Ethnography* 35, no. 4 (2006): 466–78.

the Layene community and finally agree on when I could visit the shrine. This preparation was rendered necessary because of my identity as a Roman Catholic. Not being a member of the Layene community, undertaking the pilgrimage without seeking the permission of the members of the community would have been socially inappropriate in the Senegalese context, where harmonious relations between different faith communities are actively sought and maintained.

As I prepared to visit the shrine, I viewed my Catholic identity as a source of both opportunities and challenges. Regarding opportunities, as a fellow person of faith, I could encounter the Layene within more or less shared plausibility structures. This was particularly useful in assessing the narratives I listened to when interviewing those who had come to pray at the shrine. Their interpretation of Islamic history might not stand the test of historical criticism. However, these narratives clearly structure the life of the community, giving my interlocutors a sense of belonging. The said narratives are consequently important in shaping their identity as Layene. My ability to listen to these narratives without rejecting them forthrightly was fostered by the fact that I belong to a faith community in which some of the narratives that structure the life of the community and foster identity building may, similarly, not necessarily pass the test of historical criticism.

However, being a Catholic equally made me anticipate some challenges. For instance, I wondered to what extent my hosts would allow me to partake in their rituals. Also, would there be limits regarding where I could enter? More precisely, would I be able to get into the cliffside cave? These apprehensions made me aware of how much the quality of my experience at the shrine would depend on the hospitality of my hosts. I was preparing to enter a space that has been structured by the foundational narratives of a community to which I do not belong, a space in which there are rules regarding one's behavior. To what extent would I be welcome?

The Senegalese pride themselves on being a hospitable people. This hospitality is expressed in the Wolof word *terànga* (hospitality). It is the cultural glue of the Senegalese social contract. In a 2006 survey, when asked about the perceived reasons for the harmonious relations between faith communities in Senegal, 31.6 percent indicated that it was *terànga*; 25 percent said it was *kalante* (a joking relationship); 14.5 percent said it was kinship and marriage; 11.2 percent responded that religion itself was a contributing factor (the piety of both Muslims and Christians); 3.2 percent saw the existence of a unifying language (Wolof) as a factor of social cohesion; and so on. Responses such as "understanding," "peace," "respect," and "the role of Senghor," the first president, made up the rest of the indicators given as contributing to harmonious relations between communities.[16]

Terànga was on display in the warm welcome I received at the shrine. The smiles of those who welcomed me, the chair I was offered, the cup of tea, the cordial conversation. All these made me feel welcome and wiped away some of my apprehensions. When my hosts had ascertained who I was and what my intentions were, I could see their own hesitations equally give way, paving the path for a fruitful experience at the shrine. I will dwell on three articulations of my time there: the *salat* (Muslim normative prayer), the visit to the cave, and placing my feet into the carved footprints of Seydina Limamou Laye.

---

16. See Etienne Smith, "Religion, Ethnicity and the State: The Triadic Configuration of Tolerance," in *Tolerance, Democracy, and Sufis in Senegal*, ed. Mamadou Diouf (New York: Columbia University Press, 2013), 149–51.

Salat

Soon after my arrival at the shrine, it was time for *salat*. I sat in a corner while my hosts prayed. This was the first moment of awareness of the limits of my ritual participation in this context. This had me thinking of an account of David Brown, a Christian scholar of Islam, about his experience in Khartoum:

> My distance from Islam came home to me in a sad but profound way one evening in Khartoum, when I went to the home of a Muslim leader. There were some thirty men sitting at ease in his courtyard and for an hour or more we enjoyed a good and open discussion about religious matters. The time came for the night prayer, and they formed ranks to say it together. I asked if I might stand with them, but the Sheikh told me I could not do so, since I did not have the right "intention" (*niyya*). I had to remain standing at the edge of the courtyard. Even though I have walked on the approaches of Islam for over thirty years I can only speak of it as a stranger.[17]

Had my hosts offered that I join them, I am not certain of what my response would have been. One thing was, however, clear to me. No matter how hospitable my hosts were, as I delicately moved in the sacred space of a religious community to which I did not belong, there would always be an insurmountable distance between my hosts and me. I could perform the *salat* ritual, but it would be devoid of meaning because I will lack the *niyya*. At that

---

17. D. Brown, "Meeting Muslims," in *The Churches and Islam in Europe (II)*, quoted in *Ritual Participation and Interreligious Dialogue: Boundaries, Transgressions and Innovations*, ed. Marianne Moyaert and Joris Geldof (New York: Bloomsbury, 2015), 6.

moment, abolishing the distance between us would have required that I cross the Rubicon, becoming a Muslim. This was not an option. The experience of this distance and the inner tension it carries have to be integrated into the research process. This distance is not, in itself, a bad thing. It offers a kind of "epistemological abyss" that can be a springboard for scientific objectivity.

The Cave

After the *salat*, I had a lengthy conversation with my hosts while enjoying some lemon tea. They very graciously answered all my questions and showed much interest in my research project as well as in me as an individual. Not quite sure if it was out of place, I timidly asked if I could go down into the cave where the spirit of the Prophet Muhammad is said (according to the Layene) to have been dormant for centuries before being reincarnated in Seydina Limamou Laye. They enthusiastically accepted. Despite this permission, as I went down the ladder leading into the cave, I could not help but wonder if I was violating the sacred grounds of a community.

The waves of the ocean pour into the cave. My guide told me to allow the water to touch me as a sign of blessing. I met other devotees in the cave who had come to offer prayers. I was not sure about what to do. I silently prayed in my heart even though I can no longer remember what I asked for. Throughout my time in the cave, I experienced an eerie feeling. After climbing out of the cave, I remained silent for some time, with a sense of inner calm and peace. I walked around, taking in the experience as well as the cool evening breeze from the ocean.

Many come to this cave to pray for various intentions and ask the guardian of the shrine, a grandson of Limamou Laye, to offer prayers on their behalf. Some pray to get a spouse, others to get a job, others again to be successful in business or for healing. The *baraka* (blessing) of Seydina Limamou Laye dwells there and attracts people to it. There is, to borrow Benjamin Soares's expression, the development of a "prayer economy" around the shrine—that is, the exchange of gifts for blessings, prayers, and intercession.[18] This prayer economy is a microcosm of the Senegalese macrocosm. In effect, charismatic religious figures hold a lot of sway within Senegalese society. It is common to find the name of a prominent Sufi leader given to a pharmacy or a shop or their image on display within business places or private homes. It is equally common to encounter people wearing talismans received from their religious leader. While at the shrine, I somehow took an active part in this prayer economy by offering a gift, but I did not ask for a blessing in return.

The Footprints of "Baye Laye"

The shrine of Xóotoum Ngor is equally home to a stone in which are carved footprints that are said to be those of "Baye Laye" (Father Laye), as the Layene affectionately call Seydina Limamou Laye. It is a source of blessing to place one's feet into these footprints that point in the direction of the qibla—that is, the direction of the Kaaba, which Muslims face when performing the *salat*. I squatted and placed my feet into the footprints of Baye Laye, with one knee in the sand. This seems to be the only position in which one's feet can comfortably be placed in the carved footprints. These footprints are the closest one comes to touching Baye Laye. There is no picture of his, in line with the Islamic tradition of eschewing figural representations of prophetic (saintly) figures.

---

18. See Benjamin F. Soares, *Islam and the Prayer Economy: History and Authority in a Malian Town* (Edinburgh: Edinburgh University Press, 2005), 153–80.

The footprints and the shrine in its entirety constitute a *lieu de mémoire*.[19] It is a locus where memory crystallizes and secretes itself. As all *lieux de mémoire*, this shrine is the expression of a will to remember, and it is an essential component in the definition of Layene identity. However, memory here is not turned toward the past. Rather, the past is made present through the enduring *baraka* of the founder of the community that perpetuates this charism in the present age.

Conclusion

Applied to the study of pilgrimages, autoethnography makes room for the experience of the researcher in connection with broader sociocultural and religious themes. Without the integration of this experience, ethnographic research runs the risk of missing out on the rich data that come with the fact that the researcher is not a mere spectator but rather an active participant in the phenomenon they study. Without the connection to broader sociocultural and religious themes, the ethnographic account runs the risk of simply being biographical, lacking the critical analysis that makes a research project relevant for the broader field of anthropology. However, because it relies mainly on the researcher's experience, autoethnography (at least in its evocative form) runs the risk of being limited in its conclusions.

This said, autoethnography presents tremendous opportunities for the study of pilgrimages by virtue of the very nature of the phenomenon studied, which requires that the researcher undertake the pilgrimage that constitutes the focus of their study.

---

19. See Pierre Nora, ed., *Les Lieux de Mémoire* (Paris: Gallimard, 1984–92).

Questions for Reflection

1. Have you ever been on pilgrimage to a site sacred to a community whose beliefs you do not necessarily share? If yes, how has your "distance" from the community impacted your pilgrimage experience?
2. Are you aware of what you bring (your interior life) to your research and how that interacts with the work you do, particularly in the ethnographic study of pilgrimages?
3. How do you relate to the material culture of a pilgrimage site you are studying? How much does that factor into your experience?

Select Annotated Bibliography

Adams, Tony E., Stacy Holman Jones, and Carolyn Ellis. *Handbook of Autoethnography*. London: Routledge, 2013.

This reference volume brings together dozens of thinkers and practitioners of autoethnography spanning four continents and a dozen disciplines. It covers the scope, opportunities, and challenges of autoethnography. It includes examples that show the use of the principles expounded in the volume.

Bochner, Arthur P., and Carolyn Ellis. *Evocative Autoethnography: Writing Lives and Telling Stories*. Writing Lives: Ethnographic Narratives 17. New York: Routledge, 2016.

Pioneers of evocative autoethnography, the authors present it here both as a methodology and as a way of life in the human sciences. They use examples drawn from their work and others' to show how to connect intellectually and emotionally to the lives of readers throughout the challenging process of representing lived experiences. This can be a useful handbook.

Chang, Heewon. *Autoethnography as Method*. New York: Routledge, 2016.

    The author guides the reader through the process of conducting and producing an autoethnographic study through the understanding of self, other, and culture. In addition to its theoretical contribution, its richness lies in the series of hands-on steps for data collection, analysis, and interpretation with self-reflective writing exercises that will enable the student to produce an autoethnographic work.

Hammoudi, Abdellah. *A Season in Mecca: Narrative of a Pilgrimage*. 1st American ed. New York: Hill and Wang, 2006.

    The author offers an autoethnography of his pilgrimage to Mecca. He set out for the pilgrimage desiring to both observe the hajj as an anthropologist and experience it as a mere pilgrim with the view of writing about it for both a Muslim and a non-Muslim audience.

Joyce, Janine. "Ashram Pilgrimage and Yogic Peace Education Curriculum Development: An Autoethnographic Study." *Journal of Peace Education* 17, no. 3 (2020): 263–282.

    The author offers an account of the autoethnographic study of a four-year ashrama pilgrimage and its outcome, notably the elaboration of a new peace education framework.

Scriven, Richard. "Journeying with: Qualitative Methodological Engagements with Pilgrimage." *Area (London 1969)* 51, no. 3 (2019): 540–548.

The author deploys autoethnography in the study of a walking pilgrimage on the mountain Croagh Patrick in Ireland. He shows how the use of autoethnography leads to new insights into pilgrimage experiences.

Chapter 10

This Is the Way

Faculty on the Camino de Santiago

Benjamin I. Boone and James P. Barber
College of William & Mary

Introduction: The Camino de Santiago

For nearly a millennium, pilgrims have made their way to Santiago de Compostela to visit the tomb of Saint James. These pilgrims initially journeyed from the Iberian Peninsula and then greater Europe, establishing over a dozen routes to reach the northwestern city in modern-day Galicia, a province of Spain. These routes followed established pathways connecting urban hubs, ports, and trade channels. While the number of pilgrims rose steadily in the Middle Ages through the Renaissance, the popularity of pilgrimage mirrored that of the Catholic Church and began to wane with the onset of the Enlightenment. It is not until the late twentieth century that we begin to see the Camino's revitalization and then a boom in participation in the first decades of this century.

In the fifteen years between 2004 and 2019, the Pilgrim's Office saw an increase in the number of pilgrims making the trek along the route. This office is responsible for receiving pilgrims when they arrive in Santiago and verifying that they have made a pilgrimage that qualifies for the Compostela. In 2004, 179,944 pilgrims completed the Camino and registered with the Pilgrim's Office. By 2019, the number of pilgrims and their motivations increased dramatically. The Pilgrim's Office welcomed 347,578 pilgrims in 2019, a 93 percent increase from 2004. These numbers represent only those pilgrims who complete the Camino and register at the Pilgrim's Office. Not counted here are the pilgrims who begin their journey and cannot complete it or those who arrive in Santiago and for whatever reason do not register their journey with the church.

In this latest resurgence, a majority of pilgrims use the Camino Francés, which served as the principal pathway for pilgrims arriving from across Europe into modern-day Spain. This eight-hundred-kilometer trek begins at the French and Spanish border and stretches across northern Spain. Upon arrival in Santiago de Compostela, pilgrims often procure the Compostela from the Catholic Church. This ancient document serves as proof of the pilgrim's journey. The church sets expectations for the Compostela that correlate to the manner in which a pilgrim traveled to Santiago. Those who arrive on foot must walk at least the final one hundred kilometers of their chosen route; this mandatory distance varies for pilgrims who arrive via bicycle or horseback.

There is no doubt that many pilgrims begin their journey along the Camino with the end in mind—arrival in Santiago and procurement of the Compostela. While the end is a critical and culminating experience, pilgrims ultimately share that the journey itself holds significant meaning. As they make their journeys, pilgrims stay in communal housing, share meals, and form important social bonds with fellow pilgrims. These acts and these relationships form the basis of a distinct Camino culture.

In this chapter, we provide background and insights for university faculty who want to take students on the Camino as part of a study abroad program. While this chapter focuses on the faculty leaders of these study abroad programs, we also discuss how students experience Camino study abroad programs, particularly through the lenses of disciplinary learning outcomes and student perceptions of spirituality. First, we examine the ways in which faculty members approach leading the pilgrimage. We achieve this through examining faculty motivations, professional identities, and pedagogical goals. This includes drawing on lessons learned from our personal experiences designing and teaching study abroad programs that incorporate the Camino. Then we offer insight into the pedagogical practices faculty leaders employ to teach both academic course content and the practice of pilgrimage. Throughout the chapter, we share personal reflections on our own experiences teaching courses while leading students on pilgrimage along the Camino de Santiago.

US Study Abroad on the Camino

The first study abroad program documented in the United States was launched in 1923. Raymond Kirkbride, a University of Delaware French instructor, arranged for a group of his students to spend their junior year in France. This program, now hosted by Sweet Briar College, has run nearly every year since 1923 with the exception of the years of the Second World War. As the decades progressed, study abroad in the United States became more popular, particularly for language-based programs. The United States eventually grew into the world leader for international study. The Fulbright Act of 1946, the Fulbright-Hays Act of 1961, and the Marshall Plan all helped establish and perpetuate global study as a part of American higher education.

In 1974, David Gitlitz of Indiana University led the first group of US-based college students on a study abroad program that incorporated the Camino. Unlike Kirkbride's initial cohort, Gitlitz's seven students were all women. They spent two months hiking from the border of France and Spain across the northern Iberian Peninsula to Santiago de Compostela. During the two-month journey, students had to interpret Spanish army maps, blaze their own pathways through fields and towns, and participate in class discussions on Francoist culture, medieval pilgrimage, and Spanish life. This program in 1974 set the stage for future faculty to take their students along the Camino as a means of experiential global education.

The nearly five decades between the first study abroad program and the writing of this chapter witnessed remarkable growth in the number and diversity of study abroad programs that incorporate the Camino de Santiago. As of 2019, over thirty universities in the United States offered some sort of Camino-based educational experience. These institutions represent the vast diversity of higher education in the United States. There are programs run by two-year community colleges, small liberal arts colleges, military schools, art institutes, religiously affiliated schools, public and private universities, and large flagship state institutions.

Just as diverse as the sponsoring institutions are the programs themselves. Some programs follow in Gitlitz's footsteps—literally—and walk the eight-hundred-kilometer trail from the Pyrenees to Santiago. Other programs seek out less-developed routes, such as the Camino Portugués, which travels northward from Lisbon, or the Camino Primitivo, which treks up and down the mountain ranges across the north of Spain. There are also programs that do not involve walking the Camino; rather, students take buses and trains on various routes to visit key cities along the Way. Our own Camino study abroad program begins at the end, in Santiago. We take a train to León and then walk the three hundred kilometers back to Santiago de Compostela.

The Camino has emerged as a popular destination for US study abroad programs. What does this mean for the faculty who lead students on the Camino? There are clear differences between traditional programs that place students in homestays with families or in host-university residence halls. In these programs, faculty directors would typically teach one or two classes and perhaps arrange for weekend excursions. With Camino programs, faculty directors engage in a much more complex venture. Faculty fulfill multiple roles—providing housing, food, logistics, first aid, counseling—all while also serving in the traditional faculty role of delivering academic content. The next section addresses some of the complexities faculty face when they choose to take students on the Camino and how faculty can prepare to lead such programs.

Leading a Pilgrimage as Study Abroad

As faculty begin their preparations for leading students on the Camino, there are important considerations to undertake. This section will address faculty preparation to lead a Camino study abroad program. We begin with an overview of teaching and learning frameworks that guided our own preparation and the design of our program. Then we discuss faculty motivations for engaging the Camino. These motivations drive faculty in both their personal and professional choices related to pilgrimage and study abroad. We move to a discussion of the physical and social preparation faculty undertake to lead these programs. We base much of this discussion on our own experiences leading Camino programs and the connections we have made with faculty over the years who have shared their experiences. Finally, we address student preparation—how we as faculty ensure our students are ready for the pilgrimage experience.

Study abroad students from William & Mary relax in front of the Cathedral of Santiago at the conclusion of their pilgrimage along the Camino in 2019. Photo by James P. Barber.

Frameworks for Teaching and Learning on the Camino

Two theoretical frameworks served as foundations for our experiences as faculty members on pilgrimage: James P. Barber's integration of learning and Marcia B. Baxter Magolda's self-authorship. These two models, rooted in developmental theory, guided our approach to constructing a holistic educational experience for our students (and ourselves).

At the heart of integration of learning is the notion that students thrive when they connect what they are learning across contexts.[1] Barber's initial study found that college students used three main approaches to integrate their learning, listed here in order of increasing complexity: connection, application, and synthesis. Connection is a recognition of similarity, perhaps a fleeting reminder of a previous experience or knowledge. Application is more involved and is characterized by a student using the knowledge and skills learned in one context in another context. Finally, synthesis is the most complex form of integration. It involves bringing together ideas learned in two or more contexts to form a new insight or way of seeing the world. We used this framework of integration to conceptualize our study abroad experience and encourage students to use connection, application, and synthesis throughout the program. We believed strongly that students' prior knowledge, the three courses we taught in the program, their larger academic majors in college, the cultural experience in Spain, and our pilgrimage on the Camino de Santiago needed to be integrated in order to deliver a cohesive and meaningful learning experience.

---

1. James P. Barber, *Facilitating the Integration of Learning: Five Research-Based Practices to Help College Students Connect Learning across Disciplines and Lived Experience* (Sterling, VA: Stylus, 2020).

The theory of self-authorship was also influential in the construction of our study abroad program. Self-authorship is a human developmental model that has broad appeal in higher education. It is part of a larger model of development across the life span created by Robert Kegan, the orders of consciousness. Self-authorship, popularized by Baxter Magolda's work focused on college student development, posits that people are on a journey from external frameworks, in which meaning is dictated by authorities, to internal foundations, where meaning is created by oneself.[2] Baxter Magolda found that students developed toward self-authorship in three domains: epistemological (how they see the world around them), intrapersonal (how they see themselves), and interpersonal (how they see themselves in relationships with others).

The three domains of development in Baxter Magolda's model mapped onto our program of study quite well. The epistemological domain correlated with a course we offered on regional and cultural contexts of the Camino de Santiago, the intrapersonal domain matched with the course on identity and pilgrimage, and the interpersonal domain included the *communitas*, or sense of community, encountered with other pilgrims as we walked along the way.

The frameworks of integration of learning and self-authorship complemented one another and, when taken together, informed our efforts to create a holistic study abroad experience that would join traditional academic courses and embed them within our lived experience of a three-hundred-kilometer pilgrimage.

Faculty Preparation

For most faculty, leading students on pilgrimage is unlike any other faculty role they engage on their home campuses. Faculty must

---

2. Marcia B. Baxter Magolda, *Authoring Your Life: Developing an Internal Voice to Navigate Life's Challenges* (Sterling, VA: Stylus, 2009).

physically prepare to walk at least one hundred kilometers while carrying their belongings. In addition to the typical pilgrim physical demands, faculty must also prepare mentally for leading students. Student-faculty relationships will be quite different on the Camino from on campus. We explore how these relationships unfold and ways that faculty can embrace the Camino culture while still serving as the academic authority in the program.

Motivations

In his 2019 dissertation study, Benjamin I. Boone found that faculty program leaders drew motivation for leading these programs from both internal and external sources.[3] Faculty described internal motivations related to their personal lives and experiences. These included reflections on their faith traditions and the desire for discernment during the Camino as well as seeing the Camino as a means to achieve deeper healing and recovery from tragedy and major life transitions. While these internal motivations may be incredibly personal in nature, they carried through into the professional lives of the faculty members. This blend of personal and professional identities created a unique experience for faculty as they prepared to lead their students.

External sources of inspiration emerged around three specific areas. First, faculty expressed a desire to immerse students in an authentic Spanish environment. Faculty found that students had varied and often romanticized perceptions of Spanish society involving sangria, beaches, and a robust nightlife. They wanted students to experience Galicia and the day-to-day life within the region. A second source of inspiration related to the pedagogical

---

3. Benjamin I. Boone, "Teaching along the Way: An Ethnographic Study of Faculty Growth and Sensemaking on the Camino de Santiago" (PhD diss., William & Mary, 2019), http://dx.doi.org/10.25774/w4-drs8-nx23.

possibilities that faculty saw in teaching in a Camino program. These possibilities included different means for assessment of learning, opportunities to teach course materials in a new environment, and ways for faculty to engage the real world in their day-to-day teaching. Finally, faculty found motivation in providing a study abroad opportunity that was affordable and accessible for their students. This manifested in their careful planning of the programs to maximize financial efficiency and time spent on the Camino so that students would gain as much as possible.

Communitas and Teaching on the Camino

As we discuss above, Camino culture creates a sense of *communitas* wherein power dynamics shift and pilgrims associate as coequal members of a "Camino family." This phenomenon occurs in many contexts along the Camino. Kathleen Jenkins discusses how parents and their adult children experience shifts in responsibilities and expectations while walking the Camino.[4] Likewise, on study abroad, faculty participants in Boone's dissertation study expressed a leveling effect on the Camino. Faculty began to see students as more than just learners in a classroom. They saw them as whole persons outside the educational context.

Preparing for this shift in social dynamics is important for faculty considering leading a program on the Camino. Faculty should understand that on the trail, they will be with their students constantly, oftentimes sharing space in ways that would rarely if ever happen on a college campus. As we have spent time with students on the Camino, we have come to embrace these opportunities to get to know students in a deeper way that enriches our pedagogical work. Faculty should embrace students as colearners along the Camino

---

4. Kathleen E. Jenkins, *Walking the Way Together: How Families Connect on the Camino de Santiago* (Oxford: Oxford University Press, 2021).

and help them find deeper meaning in the academic and physical work of the Camino study abroad program. The next section highlights how faculty can help students prepare for this undertaking.

Student Preparation

A key role for faculty leaders is to prepare their students to embark on a Camino journey. Much like in their own preparation, faculty orient students' thinking toward the physical demands of walking as well as newly negotiated social spaces. In this section, we provide recommendations based on our own experiences preparing students. These preparations also include managing expectations for relationships with technology and for academic engagement during the pilgrimage. We also address the role that spirituality played in our students' experiences on the Camino.

Students in our study abroad program enrolled in a one-credit academic course in the semester prior to our pilgrimage. In this course, we had four distinct objectives: (a) introduce the concept of pilgrimage and position it within the context of Spain, (b) prepare students for the physical aspects of hiking the Camino de Santiago pilgrimage route, (c) explain the uses and formats of a learning portfolio, which was our central assignment for the program, and (d) develop a sense of community among the group of student-pilgrims and faculty. We met as a group seven times before we traveled to Spain, including one class meeting that was an early morning practice hike around campus and the local community to model and foreshadow the ways that we would soon interact on our journey. These preprogram connections were critical in establishing trust with our students. We recognized that when they enroll in our program, students are putting their trust in us to provide a safe and meaningful structure unlike any learning experience they have encountered on campus. In addition to the goals mentioned above, we also helped students acquire the necessary equipment for the program, oftentimes coordinating field trips with university-owned vans for students who did not have their own cars on campus. The intense involvement we had with our students in preparing for the program created the necessary trust and confidence that was critical for a successful Camino program.

Equally important to preparing students physically for the Camino is preparing them mentally for the time on the trail. We have found that preparing our students to reframe their relationship with technology while hiking helps with the transition into an immersive Camino experience. Our experience working with students on campus during the traditional academic year has taught us that students rely on technology in nearly every aspect of their lives. They use devices to establish and maintain social relationships, manage financial transactions, and complete their coursework. When we are walking the Camino with our students, they experience an interruption in their relationship with their devices that can cause some discomfort if they are not prepared for it.

Our approach to technology on the Camino is to encourage students to be as present in the experience as possible. Without mandating a policy on technology usage, we try to help students see the value in setting aside the distractions of social media, texting, and other forms of constant connection. While on the Camino, we shift our academic content delivery so that students do not have to be connected in order to engage in their coursework. Negotiating a revised relationship with technology can be challenging for some students, and recognizing that each student may have different needs related to their access to technology is important for faculty leaders. By encouraging students to be present in the world around them, we find that they are more able to engage in conversations with their peers and with other pilgrims. They also have the space to engage in deep reflection, which oftentimes connects to their orientation toward spirituality.

Spirituality on the Camino

Spirituality is not a formal part of our program or curriculum, but it certainly is a factor in our journeys with students on the Camino de Santiago. Early in our preparation and introductions, some students begin to share their reasons for wanting to participate in this study abroad program. For some, it is the physical challenge of walking a three-hundred-kilometer section of the ancient pilgrimage route. For others, it is a time to disconnect from their college life and reconnect with nature and themselves. Still others see the Camino as a religious pilgrimage in concert with the Catholic Church or another Christian denomination. Many students have a combination of these and other motivations.

The influence of religion and spirituality is unavoidable on a study abroad program such as the Camino de Santiago. In a literal sense, we are walking across Spain to arrive at the tomb of Saint James, one of the twelve apostles of Jesus Christ. Whether or not students have a religious background or worldview, this is the historical origin of the Camino. At each city and town along the route, there is generally at least one Catholic Church, sometimes several, and all offer daily Pilgrims' Masses to welcome those passing through on their way to Santiago and offer them a blessing. As we wrote earlier in this chapter, many pilgrims register with the Pilgrim's Office (operated by the Catholic diocese) to obtain their Compostela as evidence of their journey.

The approach to spirituality in our program is to encourage discussion of multiple worldviews, religions, and ways of making meaning. We acknowledge the overt religiosity of the Catholic influences and invite students who share Christian religious beliefs and those who do not to enter into conversation about their individual perspectives. We invite students to participate in church services as cultural celebrations but do not require it. Often in our program, these shared experiences lead to in-depth, respectful conversations about students' beliefs and critiques of religion.

Critical Religious Pluralism

In considering the delivery of an academic program to an audience with diverse worldviews, critical religious pluralism theory (CRPT) is a useful tool to consider. Exploring the historical and contemporary ways that religion has been used to perpetuate inequality is essential in an experience like the Camino that centers on both the individual and collective journeys of pilgrims over time. Students are often curious about how their own religious or spiritual backgrounds connect with the millennia-long traditions of the pilgrimage to Santiago.

In our group, paintings and sculptures we encountered portraying Saint James as Matamoros, a legendary figure who miraculously appeared to assist Catholics in conquering the Muslim Moors, prompted discussions about religious persecution, privilege, and power in terms of worldviews. Some students were surprised to see violent and racist depictions in religious art; others noted connections to current discussions of social justice and antiracism. Jenny L. Small's critical religious pluralism theory and her earlier work examining faith frames (which include atheist and agnostic college students) are practical tools for guiding students in dialogue about their own personal faiths and worldviews and the larger narratives about religious pluralism.[5]

---

5. Jenny L. Small, *Critical Religious Pluralism in Higher Education: A Social Justice Framework to Support Religious Diversity* (New York: Routledge, 2020).

Just as faculty must prepare physically to lead and participate in the pilgrimage to Santiago, they also need to prepare mentally and emotionally to engage students in conversations about faith, religion, and worldview. Amanda Armstrong found that college educators' awareness of worldview diversity has a great deal of influence on student engagement with these topics. She noted that students' level of comfort discussing their experiences of religious prejudice or discrimination was often entangled with educators' own awareness (or unawareness) of bias and inequity related to worldview.[6] Educators who have the capacity to promote pluralism and interfaith engagement may create a more favorable environment for students to do the same.

Reflection as Spirituality

One of the ways that we encouraged a pluralistic spirituality on the Camino de Santiago was through formal and informal opportunities for reflection. Prayer, meditation, yoga, and free-writing are all ways in which students and faculty may choose to reflect. We encouraged students to reflect in a way that was meaningful and comfortable to them, and we were intentional in establishing time for reflection in our formal and informal activities. In more formal class experiences, we often reserved ten to fifteen minutes for written reflection. In less formal group meetings or conversations as we were walking "the Way," we asked students to think and process information for a few minutes before talking. Students of course had their own ways of reflecting as well, including drawing, listening to music, and studying religious texts. The ways in which students reflected were not as important as the practice of

6. Amanda R. Armstrong, "'It Put Me in a Really Uncomfortable Situation': A Need for Critically Conscious Educators in Interworldview Efforts," *Journal of College and Character* 20, no. 2 (2019), http://dx.doi.org/10.1080/2194587x.2019.1591287.

reflection. Students (and faculty) need intentional time to reflect in study abroad experiences such as this where they are examining multiple perspectives that may conflict with their previous ways of thinking. It is important to acknowledge that faculty on the Camino are physically and mentally challenged in a manner that is different from their normal teaching in a campus setting; reflection is essential for them to be able to process their own experiences and support their students as well.

Delivering Academic Content on the Camino

In the vast majority of Camino programs hosted by US institutions, students receive academic credit for their participation. The delivery of content for these credits varies among programs. Some Camino experiences serve as a capstone to a spring semester course. Other programs choose to blend content with the Camino experience, and students receive credit for a summer course. Our own program functions in this way. We teach our own course that lasts the duration of our five-week program—including content delivery while walking the Camino.

Our content mirrors our distinct but complementary interests in the Camino. Barber's course focuses on identity development and self-authorship in the context of pilgrimage. Relying on both academic texts and works of fiction, Barber engages students in thinking about the context and growth of an individual as it relates to pilgrimage. In the second course within our program, Boone focuses on the external experiences of pilgrimage—the culture and traditions of the Camino in both historical and contemporary frameworks. The two courses together provide opportunities for students to reflect on their own experiences and constructs of self within the larger context of the Camino and the shared experience of pilgrimage.

As we designed our courses, we took into account much of what we have discussed so far in this chapter—our motivations, the unique learning environment of the Camino, and our knowledge of how students engage the world around them. Our program begins with a week of traditional, classroom-based learning in Santiago de Compostela. This involves lectures, group discussions, and field excursions to museums. As we transition to weeks two through four, our coursework shifts to a more applied focus with students reflecting on and engaging with the Camino. Finally, when we return to Santiago de Compostela, students begin to synthesize their learning and create their portfolios. These portfolios serve as a capstone to the program and integrate learning from both academic courses.

When designing the coursework associated with a study abroad program on the Camino, faculty should keep in mind the environment in which they will be teaching. Students learn differently in experiential settings, and course content and delivery methods should reflect that reality. Accounting for the unique nature of learning on the Camino, faculty have the opportunity to design and deliver engaging academic coursework that proves fulfilling for both the students and the instructor.

Conclusion

In closing, we highlight the need for more established resources on teaching students while walking the Camino. In a practical sense, faculty need nuanced support from their institutions for logistics, budgeting, and planning. Faculty also need to feel empowered to lead these programs without concern that there may be negative implications for their promotion and retention reviews. Future research should explore the ways in which students and faculty process their Camino experiences in the semesters and years following the program. This type of longitudinal examination will help us understand better how institutions can best support and prepare faculty and students for not only Camino-based programs but also other experiential global learning opportunities.

When faculty use the concept of integration of learning in developing their study abroad programs on the Camino, individual course assignments and readings synthesize with motivations, observations, and conversations along the route. Those conversations and musings while hiking become building blocks for the assignments, and perhaps the readings are fodder for dialogue with a walking partner. In this way, the educational experience becomes more than the sum of its parts, emerging as both meaningful and transformational for students.

Questions for Reflection

1. What are your personal motivations for undertaking the pilgrimage? Will the leader be able to devote time to honoring these motivations while leading a group of students?
2. What distinctive steps can pilgrims and guides take to best prepare themselves physically and emotionally before the journey?
3. In the case of a study abroad program, are there specific learning objectives that you or your institution would want to see students achieve?
4. As a leader, how would you process the experience of the journey—both personally and professionally—with your group?

Select Annotated Bibliography

Barber, James P. *Facilitating the Integration of Learning: Five Research-Based Practices to Help College Students Connect Learning across Disciplines and Lived Experience.* Sterling, VA: Stylus, 2020.

    Barber's book offers practical strategies for college educators to help students connect knowledge and insights across various contexts, experiences, and disciplinary boundaries.

Baxter Magolda, Marcia B. *Authoring Your Life: Developing an Internal Voice to Navigate Life's Challenges.* Sterling, VA: Stylus, 2009.

    This book offers a comprehensive description of the theory of self-authorship. Baxter Magolda illustrates her theory of human development by drawing upon the life stories of thirty-five individuals.

Boone, Benjamin I. "Teaching along the Way: An Ethnographic Study of Faculty Growth and Sensemaking on the Camino de Santiago." PhD diss., William & Mary, 2019. http://dx.doi.org/10.25774/w4-drs8-nx23.

    Boone's dissertation provides an understanding of how faculty who lead students on the Camino de Santiago make sense of their roles and how they engage the Camino as an educational environment.

Frey, Nancy. *Pilgrim Stories: On and off the Road to Santiago.* Berkeley: University of California Press, 1998.

    Frey's seminal work delves deep into the lives of the pilgrims and people along the Camino. Her work is the first in-depth ethnography related to the Camino de Santiago.

Jenkins, Kathleen E. *Walking the Way Together: How Families Connect on the Camino de Santiago.* Oxford: Oxford University Press, 2021.

    Jenkins explores the relationships of parents and their adult children who walk the Camino together. Chapter 4 deals with technology along the Camino.

Small, Jenny L. *Critical Religious Pluralism in Higher Education: A Social Justice Framework to Support Religious Diversity.* New York: Routledge, 2020.

    In this volume, Small details the seven tenets of her critical religious pluralism theory, developed to support religious, secular, and spiritual diversity in higher education.

Talbot, Lynn K., and Andrew Talbot Squires, eds. *Following the Yellow Arrow: Younger Pilgrims on the Camino.* Livermore, CA: WingSpan, 2011.

    This collection of essays showcases young adults' experiences on the Camino.

Chapter 11

Pilgrimage Pedagogy and Wilderness Journeys

Kip Redick

Christopher Newport University

Twenty years ago, I approached my department chair with a proposal to include students in my area of research interest: pilgrimage studies, wilderness trails, and environment, space, and place. Unaware of anyone else in the discipline of philosophy or religion who was taking students on long-distance trips in the wilderness, I began constructing a pedagogy based on my own research approach, phenomenology. As the course evolved and I added new trips—Wonderland Trail, West Highland Way, and the Camino de Santiago—new themes emerged. Through conference presentations, publishing, and meeting other researchers in the field, I learned that most other scholars were using methodologies rooted in the social sciences. My approach opened my student researchers to ethnography rooted in a participatory experience. Teaching courses along pilgrimage routes and wilderness trails involved a number of administrative and field-related challenges inherent to my situation at a public institution. This essay will outline my background, courses taught, and these challenges, both administrative and field specific. The phenomenological approach and various readings will be discussed. Themes that have emerged will be explored, including but not limited to flow, wilderness as a sacred place, tourists versus pilgrims, veterans and pilgrimage, liminality, *communitas*, hospitality, ascetic practices, walking prayer/meditation/contemplation, and connections to environmental issues.

Background

After concluding my doctoral dissertation, a focus on wilderness landscape aesthetics—the Hudson River school of painters and architecture of Frederick Law Olmsted—I looked toward potential wilderness studies. Olmsted had pointed to the health benefits of parks, and Benton MacKaye, in proposing the idea of a trail along the Appalachian Mountains, also called attention to this benefit. MacKaye writes of "the possibilities for health and recuperation. The oxygen in the mountain air along the Appalachian skyline is a natural resource (and a national resource) that radiates to the heavens its enormous health-giving powers with only a fraction of a percent utilized for human rehabilitation. Here is a resource that could save thousands of lives."[1] Olmsted's Central Park in New York City benefited those who did not have the means to escape to the mountains. MacKaye's trail would be a day's ride for people living in the east who could not afford an extended trip to the west where most of the national parks were located. Neither Olmsted nor MacKaye envisioned these resources as places for extended hikes. It was not until 1948 that Earl Shaffer walked the entire two-thousand-plus-mile Appalachian Trail in one continuous hike. Combining the ideas of saving "thousands of lives" and the extended hike, I looked to wilderness trails such as the Appalachian Trail, the Pacific Crest Trail, and the Continental Divide Trail as sites where hikers engage in a new kind of pilgrimage. I asked, Can hiking on a wilderness

1. Benton MacKaye, "An Appalachian Trail: A Project in Regional Planning," *Journal of the American Institute of Architects* 9, no. 10 (October 1921): 325–30.

trail be compared with a traditional pilgrimage, and what are the similarities and differences?

Noel Grove's article in *National Geographic*, "A Tunnel through Time: The Appalachian Trail," points to the religious aspect of this long-distance hike: "In their search for a retreat, hikers and monastics have more in common than they realize. On the trail, hikers revert to lives of simplicity, denying themselves modern comfort, seeking purification in an uncorrupted world. Monkishly, a thru-hiker from Connecticut told me that he wished somehow he could walk it indefinitely—'for the simpler life-style.'"[2] Grove's account also showed me the connection to sacred time, liminality, and *communitas*: "Foot travelers meeting, sharing shelter, exchanging food, information, and nicknames . . . had walked back in time through a tunnel of green."[3] These wilderness backpackers were like pilgrims along some medieval route in Europe, seeking what only an extended journey will allow. Like traditional pilgrims, they find fellowship and realize spiritual fulfillment. Another similarity is that "most are people at some transitional point in their lives—divorce, job change, or just self-discovery. . . . It's a pilgrimage not unlike those made in the Middle Ages."[4]

I began conducting research on the Appalachian Trail and discovered the rich meaning of this hike in the wilderness. Visiting the Appalachian Trail Conservancy in Harpers Ferry, West Virginia, I read through archives of trail registers, small notebooks placed at shelters wherein hikers write notes. These trail registers evidenced the spirituality of the journey for many hikers. Leaving Harpers Ferry, I embarked into the wilderness. Immediately, the feeling of entering an alternative world came upon me. I became liminal and

---

2. Noel Grove, "A Tunnel through Time: The Appalachian Trail," *National Geographic*, February 1987, 229.
3. Grove, 235.
4. Grove, 235.

felt removed from the highway and all its connecting webs. At the same time, a wave of nostalgia washed over me as I was thrust backward into a transitional time in my own life.

Several months after being discharged from the Marine Corps, my best friend presented a call to go on a spiritual quest. He suggested we purchase backpacks and gear in order to hike the Pacific Crest Trail. He pointed out that we were in a "spiritual rut," and the trail would provide a way out of our dilemma. We gave away all of our possessions, everything except what would fit in our packs, and began hiking. After the trail, we continued to travel, hitchhike, and live out of our packs, all the while seeking meaning in our lives. Our journey resulted in my own traverse of the continent six times as well as living on the North Shore of Hawaii in a grove of ironwood trees. Now, all these years later, the wave washing over me seemed to be the same waters in which I had bathed. The rhetoric of the trail registers was reminiscent of our quest. The trees and mountain terrain seemed to offer healing.

Back at the university, I started writing about the intersection of long-distance wilderness hiking and pilgrimage. In the wake of this scholarship and initiatives to include undergraduates in research, I approached the chair of my department and proposed a class on the Appalachian Trail. In a combined philosophy and religion department, the class would focus on religious aspects of wilderness hiking and employ a phenomenological approach. The students would engage in ethnographic research with thru-hikers and also interact with the environmental milieu.

Overview of Courses Taught

I have conducted the course Pilgrimage on the Appalachian Trail every May since 2002: eighteen trips with more than 226 students.

We enter the trail at Dennis Cove, Tennessee, targeting an area where there are many thru-hikers headed for Maine. We always start with a visit to Kincora Hostel, where the students meet thru-hikers staying there. This initial meeting is always awkward. The thru-hikers are veterans by this time, having walked from Springer Mountain, Georgia, more than four hundred miles to the south. My students perceive themselves as outsiders, and many of the thru-hikers assume we are a group of typical college students invading the trail. The hostel provides a good environment to facilitate opening ourselves up to one another. Fifty miles north and five days later, we walk across the Virginia state line and descend into Damascus. The experience of crossing a state boundary and leaving the wilderness to enter a small mountain village helps in our transition to becoming experienced hikers. In addition, the timing of the class places us in Damascus during the annual Trail Days festival. The village swells with visitors, both veteran thru-hikers from past years and people who have never hiked. The current year's thru-hikers get off the trail and hitchhike to Damascus from as far away as two hundred miles north and south. In this festival free-for-all, the students begin to perceive themselves as accomplished hikers and are better able to interact with thru-hikers. Many of the hikers who passed us on the way to Damascus are enjoying the festival, and the students engage them in further conversation.

Rather than using a methodology, we approach ethnography phenomenologically. Information gained in the first few days of hiking is enriched as a result of experience. Students begin to identify with long-distance hikers, having gone through their own initiation to the trail. After two days in Damascus, we return to the trail and begin climbing toward the Grayson Highlands, where two of Virginia's highest mountains are located. During these four days, we encounter hikers with whom we have already become acquainted.

Students now share experiences with these hikers and are better able to understand the unique hiker culture. When we arrive in Rhododendron Gap, close to five thousand feet in elevation, we set up a camp and remain for four days. During this time, students reflect on their journey, day hike, and interact with the highland ecosystem.

In 2004, I created an additional wilderness experience course wherein students interacted with the surrounding environment. We circumnavigated Mount Rainier on the Wonderland Trail. This trail is more remote than the section of the Appalachian Trail in Tennessee and Virginia. During the hike, we only entered areas frequented by people twice, at the Sunrise Visitor Center seven days into the trek and at Paradise after twelve days.

In 2006, I created a wilderness course in the Highlands of Scotland. Similar to the Wonderland Trail class, I designed it as an experiential examination of the intersection of spiritual journeys and harsh landscapes. Eleven students and I hiked for three weeks along established trails: the West Highland Way, one hundred miles; the Great Glen Way, seventy-five miles; and several shorter trails on the Isle of Skye.

In 2007, in addition to the Appalachian Trail class in Tennessee and Virginia, I proposed and taught a leadership seminar titled Crucible in the Wilderness. We hiked from Monson, Maine, to Baxter State Park, through the one-hundred-mile wilderness of the Appalachian Trail, the northernmost section terminating on top of Mount Katahdin.

I have taught six classes walking the Camino de Santiago—beginning in France and hiking across Spain to the Atlantic Ocean: 2008, 2010, 2013, 2015, 2017, and 2019 with a total of ninety students.

Several pilgrimage classes that did not involve walking have informed my continued design of wilderness journeys. In 2008, I took ten students to Rome. In the spring semester of 2016 and 2017, during spring break, I led trips to Israel.

Through all of these experiences, I have gained insight into creating and maintaining pilgrimage courses wherein walking long distances adds a unique challenge. Some of my most difficult hurdles come from administrative oversight.

Administrative Challenges

Christopher Newport University, a relatively young and small liberal arts and sciences state university, requires me to enroll a minimum of ten students. Over the years, the administration has canceled two of my classes due to low enrollments: a pilgrimage on the Camino de Santiago in 2012 with seven students and a pilgrimage in Ireland in 2014 with seven students. I am required to recruit students. The pool of philosophy majors is small, creating a necessity to recruit students from other majors who take my courses as electives. That the class requires wild camping and walking long distances with backpacks presents other recruiting hurdles. The administration requires me to identify potential students through an application process early in the fall semester. These students must secure a position in the class with a deposit of $100 by midsemester.

In order to enroll ten students, I need to approve between thirty and forty applications. This situation makes it impossible to have a cutoff of ten or even fifteen students, a workable number but still too large a group for wilderness trekking. As a result, my classes over the years have fluctuated between ten and seventeen students. I have taught the class eighteen times with an average of twelve and a half students per class. This administrative challenge puts the class at odds with a restriction on wilderness hiking. Wilderness areas restrict hiking groups to ten persons. With the minimum of ten students and two faculty members (another administrative restriction), I could never teach a course on a wilderness trail and comply with wilderness area rules. Given the administrative challenge outlined here, I decided that giving students this unique pilgrimage experience outweighs the rule of maximum numbers in the wilderness. In addition, we do not hike as a group but split up.

Course Challenges

Any long-distance hike in the wilderness involves a multitude of challenges: injuries and illness occurring miles from help, the possibility of encountering dangerous wild animals such as poisonous snakes and bears, negotiating extremely difficult terrain while carrying a heavy pack, the logistics of eating and finding water, and weather are just a few. Taking a group intensifies these hurdles. Teaching a university class focused on research that is both ethnographic and autoethnographic while employing a phenomenological approach accentuates these challenges and brings with it something unique. Phenomenology requires the student researcher to open themselves to the other as the other gives itself from itself. If the class structure employs a frame of distance designed to reduce these challenges, the student researcher will not encounter the very thing that manifests itself in a particular wilderness situation. For example, a class structure requiring students to walk in groups of three or more as a safety precaution is a frame of distance that could prevent a bear encounter, something that happens regularly on long-distance hikes in the wilderness. Or using vehicles to transport packs from a morning location to an evening location, allowing student researchers to hike without the burden of their gear, is a frame of distance that prevents the manifestation of gravity giving itself from itself as steep ascents and descents happen. If those same support vehicles provided water, student researchers would fail to find meaning in discovering springs, drawing water from streams, treating water, or becoming aware of the connection between body and environment.

Frames of distance throw light on phenomenological reduction, bracketing preconceptions or, as Jean-Luc Marion writes, "as much reduction, as much givenness."[5] Reducing frames of distance opens student researchers to the very challenges outlined. At the same time, as professor and leader of the class, I feel the burden of responsibility. If I employ frames of distance as a way of creating a "safety net," my burden of responsibility toward student safety is somewhat lifted, but I fail to allow the very encounters that make a wilderness trek meaningful and thereby fail in my responsibility as a teacher. Reducing these frames of distance will bring enhanced anxiety. Students in past years have suffered various kinds of injuries and illness, ranging from twisted ankles to norovirus. Students have had to walk as much as ten miles after severe norovirus symptoms kept them up all night. Some students decide to exit the trail at road crossings after feeling various aches and pains. Others press through. One year a student was evacuated after the first day with a very bad ankle twist. Two volunteers helped him hobble a couple of miles down a forest service road so that a local hostel owner could drive him out of the wilderness. He saw a doctor and continued for the second week of the trip, hiking on crutches while still carrying his pack. The incident caused my anxiety level to rise, but the outcome could not have been better in terms of pedagogy. All of the students in that particular class participated in this incident in some way or another. Everyone grappled with the meaning

---

5. Jean-Luc Marion, *In Excess: Studies of Saturated Phenomena*, trans. Robyn Horner and Vincent Berraud (New York: Fordham University Press, 2002), 17.

of long-distance hiking as it made itself manifest through a fellow being injured, requiring aid and assistance, and then persevering.

Very few hikers enjoy walking through the wilderness during inclement weather. The trail becomes muddy or even turns into a stream. Everything gets wet, even with the best rain gear. Day hikers or weekend backpackers opt to cut their journeys short and go home. Long-distance hikers must continue through the rain, sleet, fog, or wind. The aphorism "No rain, no pain, no Maine" resounds along the Appalachian Trail and showers hikers with the truth that in order to accomplish the journey, enduring hardships of a variety of weather conditions is necessary. Student researchers learn this truth through experiencing these conditions firsthand. Some of my students have slept in wet sleeping bags, walked all day long through constant rain, been buffeted by strong winds, and endured very cold nights.

Coordinating the necessary backpacking gear is also a challenge, especially in the context of a public university wherein purchasing equipment for such a class is an impossibility. Students must supply their own equipment, and many of our students do not have it within their limited budget to purchase expensive gear. I identify the basic necessities, like a backpack with a hip belt ($150–$200), a lightweight sleeping bag that has at least a twenty-five-degree rating ($100–$200), an insulation pad ($20–$50), footwear ($80–$150), moisture-wicking socks ($10–$20 a pair), water containers ($10–$30), a cooking pot ($10–$100), rain gear ($40–$300), waterproof sacks for clothing and food ($30–$70), and clothing that is not cotton. Optional items include a tent, water filter or treatment, and other miscellaneous pieces. If students cannot afford a tent, I coordinate sharing opportunities: a student with a two-person tent can share the weight and space with a student without. If half the class has water filters or treatment, those with can share. I conduct a stove-making workshop at my home. For those who cannot afford an expensive stove, I help them make "beer-can stoves," a very light-weight option that burns alcohol. The stove is free and the alcohol costs about a dollar for twelve ounces, enough for a week on the trail.

Research and Pedagogy Approach

I employ a phenomenological approach and introduce it to students as we hike in the wilderness. Pilgrimage as a *liminal* journey and wilderness as a *liminal* space open themselves to the researcher who carefully employs this approach. Maurice Merleau-Ponty's phenomenological description shows the possibility of bracketing conceptual frames that other methodologies employ, recognizing our human tendency to schematize the things we study, and opening ourselves to the other or the wild that appears from beyond our projection: "To turn back to the things themselves is to return to that world prior to knowledge of which knowledge speaks."[6] He goes on to write, "The real must be described and not constructed or constituted."[7] I teach my student researchers to attend to their descriptions, setting aside constructions or conceptualizations of their encounters. Our class's turning to the wild becomes a gesture of opening ourselves to the world of things that exist beyond our conceptual framing. Phenomenologists attempt to discover such a world of things, as do many hikers/pilgrims who venture out on the Appalachian Trail or many other pilgrimage routes. A phenomenological approach in the context of a pilgrimage in the wilderness opens both the one who seeks wildness (or pilgrimage to a sacred

---

6. Maurice Merleau-Ponty, "What Is Phenomenology?," *Cross Currents* 6, no. 2 (1956): 60.
7. Merleau-Ponty, 61.

place) and the student researcher to discover it giving itself from beyond sedimented and conceptualized experience.

Themes often prevent a return to the world prior to knowledge, as they are themselves a form of sedimented knowledge, creating a filter through which "that world prior to knowledge" is schematized and thereby conceptualized. This is an important caution given in light of the phenomenological approach. Though themes do rise through phenomenological description, the description should not be framed by themes. In this way, discussions focused on careful phenomenological description look for themes that rise in light of the phenomenon giving itself and discover meaning through a hermeneutic interplay among the given, the giver, and the one describing. The following interaction with some of those themes rising from pilgrimage in the wilderness will be explored in this light, and I will also interact with the readings used by the class in the hermeneutic interplay.

Themes and Readings

Some of the themes that emerge during our phenomenological exploration of pilgrimage on the Appalachian Trail are liminality, flow or kenotic walking, *communitas*, veterans and healing, wilderness as sacred space, hospitality, the identity of tourist versus pilgrim, ascetic practices, walking prayer/meditation/contemplation, and environmental issues. What follows is a brief interaction with some of these themes and a mention of some of the readings used.

Liminality

One theoretical frame for understanding pilgrimage thematizes it as a ritual action. Yet ritual action becomes problematic in our contemporary situation wherein not all pilgrims engage in the practice through religion or spirituality. Interacting with pilgrims both religious and other than religious reveals a complex relationship between the pilgrim and ritual.[8] In addition to religious ritual action, liminality can also be interpreted through play and thereby become inclusive of religious and other-than-religious participants. I employ Johan Huizinga's *Homo Ludens: A Study of the Play-Element in Culture* to explore play in this way. He writes, "Ritual grew up in sacred play."[9] Paul Shepard writes that play is "an alternative to everyday utilitarian activities. To 'go out to play' is to go out of the banal envelope of the daily routine of the adults, to leave the system of profane rules."[10] Huizinga points out that this is happening in a bounded space: "All play moves and has its being within a playground marked off. . . . Just as there is no formal difference between play and ritual, so the 'consecrated spot' cannot be formally distinguished from the play-ground."[11] Such bounded spaces are *liminal* and ephemeral: "All are temporary worlds within the ordinary world, dedicated to the performance of an act apart."[12] *Liminal* space manifests itself in religious and other-than-religious persons engaged in a similar journey, all of whom are separated from ordinary life: "One of the most important characteristics of play was its spatial separation from ordinary life."[13]

---

8. Introducing liminality, I use Victor and Edith Turner's study of pilgrimage, *Image and Pilgrimage in Christian Culture* (New York: Columbia University Press, 1978), as well as two other books by Victor Turner: *Dramas, Fields, and Metaphors: Symbolic Action in Human Society* (Ithaca: Cornell University Press, 1974); and *The Ritual Process: Structure and Anti-structure* (Ithaca: Cornell University Press, 1977).

9. Johan Huizinga, *Homo Ludens: A Study of the Play-Element in Culture* (Boston: Beacon, 1950), 173.

10. Paul Shepard, *Man in the Landscape: A Historic View of the Esthetics of Nature* (College Station: Texas A&M University Press, 1967), 197.

11. Huizinga, *Homo Ludens*, 10.

12. Huizinga, 10.

13. Huizinga, 19.

Spatial separation manifests as students traverse
the Roan Highlands. Photo by the author.

Liminal space also reveals pilgrimage as a kind of phenomenological journey. Considering Marion's proposed connection between
reduction and givenness,[14] reduction distances one from the natural
attitude, setting aside ordinary lived experience and opening to the
given. *Liminal* space becomes a setting of reduction. *Liminal* space
creates a gap in which the given both gives itself and is received in
an interaction of hospitality, "between the (appearing, transcendent)
thing and (immanent) lived experience (in which the thing would
appear)."[15] Liminality opens the hiker/pilgrim to an alternative attitude, the attitude of their body ascending a steep slope while discovering communion with the boulders along the path. This also points
to an alternative to a social understanding of *liminality*; pilgrims

14. Marion, *In Excess*, 17.
15. Marion, 55.

discover communion with the other, human and extrahuman. One example of alternative attitude happens in flow.

Flow

Victor and Edith Turner write that pilgrimages "provide eminently satisfactory frames for the flow experience, in both the journey to and the exercises at the pilgrimage center. Asceticism has its joys—the joys of flow. And flow can serve to reinforce the symbols and values with which its frames are associated."[16] My own published research also finds its way into these classes, and in the case of flow, I write, "When flow happens, the pilgrim's full attention is focused on the present moment and their full awareness encompasses all of the particular constituents of the surrounding milieu."[17] Mihaly Csikszentmihalyi writes, "One is very aware of one's actions, but not of the awareness itself."[18] Walking flow shifts awareness beyond self-consciousness. I call this kenotic walking or walking self-emptying. This kind of walking opens the hiker/pilgrim to an "embodied dialogue wherein the phenomenological given gives fully in the gap between itself as transcendent and the pilgrim's (immanent) lived experience."[19]

Ascetic Practices

In my own lived experience, my most significant ascetic practices were, first, Marine Corps recruit training; second, requiring more self-discipline, my PhD program; and the most challenging, my

---

16. Turner and Turner, *Image and Pilgrimage*, 139.
17. Kip Redick, "The Connection between Liminal Places and Hospitality in Manifesting Pilgrim Values and Identity," in *Pilgrim Values and Identity*, ed. Darius Liutikas, CABI, Religious Tourism and Pilgrimage Series (Vilnius: Lithuanian Social Research Centre, 2021), 41.
18. Mihaly Csikszentmihalyi, "Play and Intrinsic Rewards," *Journal of Humanistic Psychology* 15, no. 3 (1975): 45.
19. Redick, "Manifesting Pilgrim Values and Identity," 41.

sabbatical thru-hike of the Appalachian Trail. Long-distance hiking in the wilderness requires an excess of self-discipline and a combination of ascetic practices. Students experience this ascetic practice and interview many long-distance hikers who are in the midst of their own practice. Turner and Turner write in relation to the *askesis* of pilgrimage, "The weariness of the body is submitted to hard, voluntary discipline, loosening the bonds of matter to liberate the spirit."[20] In my article "Spiritual Rambling," I write,

> Like pilgrims, long distance hikers give up comfortable shelters, beds, fashionable clothing, hot showers, culinary delights, and toilets just to name a few things. They submit themselves to long, hard, solitary walks through weather conditions that most people would avoid. Theirs is not a gnostic denial of the value of embodiment, a turning to spirit in exclusion of the physical, as spirit somehow being the real beyond the illusion of the physical. Rather, it is a focused discipline whereby the hold of the marketplace is devalued, where intrinsic versus extrinsic values are emphasized, where fellows are encountered as ends in themselves rather than a means to some self-interested end.[21]

Such ascetic practices facilitate an exegesis of the participant's life story and then the scripting of an alternative narrative in the quest for meaning.

---

20. Turner and Turner, *Image and Pilgrimage*, 95.
21. Kip Redick, "Spiritual Rambling: Long Distance Wilderness Sojourning as Meaning-Making," *Journal of Ritual Studies* 30, no. 2 (2016): 47.

Conclusion

During the final four days of the Pilgrimage on the Appalachian Trail class, while camping in Rhododendron Gap, we gather for classes in the morning and evening, in addition to having informal discussions throughout each day. The student researchers begin to formulate projects. Some have identified an interest earlier in the class, but most wait and consider all of their encounters and the full array of themes that have emerged thus far. I am open to them completing a project that intertwines their major and their discoveries on the trail. I have had fine art majors complete portfolios of paintings and/or drawings to fulfill their project. After leaving the mountains, they have June and July to craft a final term paper or alternative project. Through a combination of self-discovery and ethnography, we find that a long-distance hike in the wilderness resembles a traditional religious pilgrimage requiring a trek to a sacred site.

Questions for Reflection

1. What are the similarities and differences between hiking on a wilderness trail and walking a traditional pilgrimage route?
2. How does unconditional hospitality reveal the distinction between a tourist and a pilgrim?
3. How does thematizing, schematizing, or conceptualizing prevent describing the subject giving itself from itself?

Select Annotated Bibliography

Lane, Belden C. *Backpacking with the Saints: Wilderness Hiking as Spiritual Practice.* New York: Oxford University Press, 2014.

———. *Landscapes of the Sacred: Geography and Narrative in American Spirituality.* Baltimore: Johns Hopkins University Press, 2001.

Lane's *Backpacking with the Saints* presents an interaction between a classic writing of some significant religious writer—"a saint"—and a particular trail in the wilderness. These interactions are deeply personal and meaningful. For example, in chapter 6, he explores solitude through the writings of Søren Kierkegaard and a hike in the Bell Mountain Wilderness in Missouri. These are perfect illustrations of the possibility of pilgrimage in a wilderness area. Lane's *Landscapes of the Sacred* starts with a discussion of the nature of sacred space/place. He lays out helpful axioms of such landscapes and introduces several approaches toward understanding them.

Redick, Kip. "Interpreting Contemporary Pilgrimage as Spiritual Journey or Aesthetic Tourism along the Appalachian Trail." *International Journal of Religious Tourism and Pilgrimage* 6, no. 2 (2018): 78–88.

This essay compares and contrasts two approaches to pilgrimage, tourism versus spiritual journey. Landscape aesthetics serve as a way of interpreting the difference between the approaches.

———. "Kenotic Walking, Wilderness Sojourning, and Hospitality." In "Religious Experience and Ecology," edited by Jack Hunter. Special issue, *Journal for the Study of Religious Experience* 7 no. 2 (2021): 114–139.

This essay explores wilderness walking as a practice of self-emptying. I pick up on the experience of flow as discussed in another publication and show how this decenters self and opens the hiker to the alterity of the other in fellowship.

———. "Spiritual Rambling: Long Distance Wilderness Sojourning as Meaning-Making." *Journal of Ritual Studies* 30, no. 2 (2016): 41–51.

A study of the flow experience as it relates to long-distance hiking.

———. "Wilderness as *Axis Mundi*: Spiritual Journeys on the Appalachian Trail." In *Symbolic Landscapes*, edited by Gary Backhaus and John Murungi, 65–90. London: Springer, 2009.

A study of wilderness as sacred space in the spirituality of both Old and New Testaments as relevant to long-distance hiking in the American wilderness.

Chapter 12

Healing the Broken Heart of Flint

Mary Jo Kietzman

University of Michigan-Flint

Flint, Michigan, is a damaged postindustrial city where 20 percent of the land area is industrial brownfield, where there are over thirty thousand abandoned houses, where one-third of city residents live below the poverty line, and where in fifty years, nearly 50 percent of the population has migrated out. Flint made national headlines before and during the 2016 presidential race that brought Donald Trump to power, when the city was in the throes of a water crisis in which citizens suffered lead poisoning and outbreaks of Legionella caused by state government neglect and local misgovernment by an appointed emergency manager, aging infrastructure, and the failure to listen to those with boots on the ground. But the water crisis was only the latest tragedy to befall an ailing city hit hard in the 1970s and 1980s when General Motors (GM) cut jobs and eventually closed factories in its plan to move production to the suburbs and overseas. In the decades when GM was pulling up stakes and more and more "Flintstones" were filing for unemployment, boosters moved ahead with "urban renewal" initiatives that wrecked the integrity of neighborhoods and furthered racial and economic segregation. Eventually, Vehicle City morphed into Murdertown, USA, as crime related to drug activity and gang violence rose and waves of arson swept through the streets, making Flint the nation's arson capital between 2010 and 2012.

Why take young people on pilgrimage to such a damaged and reputedly dangerous urban place? Because postindustrial blight is an all too real phenomenon, and fear of it has led to mass exoduses to suburbs and exurbs—a trend we must reverse. Instead of abandoning blighted lands, we must teach the young to love such places not despite their brokenness but because of it. There are Flints all over the United States, writes Andrew Highsmith, "in the economically depressed neighborhoods of Decatur, Illinois; Camden, New Jersey; Erie, Pennsylvania, and other struggling cities once renowned for their industrial might."[1] Flint exists in any urban place "defined more by fragmentation and exclusion than by cooperation and inclusion."[2] The crises that occur when urban systems malfunction have given rise to a dystopian form of pilgrimage. Volunteer pilgrims flocked to Flint during the water crisis, eager to distribute water, information, and do anything they could to help ease the suffering in a city dubbed "our Calcutta" by a Catholic priest from an affluent nearby city. The gathered bodies of volunteers and protestors look remarkably similar to the collection of pilgrims around holy sites.[3] The main difference is that their journeys are intentionally instrumental: they come into a city to address a crisis situation and leave, feeling good that they've helped the poor or the downtrodden. Urban pilgrimage as I envision and teach it is something indwellers do habitually and ritually; it is patterned movement that binds us to this world as it is. Urban pilgrimage is connected to prayer walks and eucharistic processions

---

1. Andrew Highsmith, *Demolition Means Progress: Flint, Michigan, and the Fate of the American Metropolis* (Chicago: University of Chicago Press, 2015), 285.
2. Highsmith, 285.
3. Lawrence Yang and Padma Maitland, "Urban Pilgrimage," *Room One Thousand*, no. 3 (2015), http://www.roomonethousand.com/introduction.

where neighbors, houses, and even barking dogs are blessed, but the goals of its practitioners are even more humble. By walking into broken urban worlds, we abandon the material and psychological securities to which we've clung and are challenged to experience our own homelessness, ugliness, resourcelessness, and spiritual poverty as prerequisites to receiving grace that comes as a surprise, a violent shock, a reversal, a gift—something utterly unexpected that wakes us up to the life of an ostensibly dead city and to our own aliveness. As one of my students said, "If one person sees more or becomes more alive, that changes the world," and that is really the only way to change the prognosis for cities like Flint.

My course for freshmen that gets students walking the city and culminates in an urban pilgrimage brings young people back to the empty center, walks them beyond stereotypes, and invites them to participate in the special significance of a city with a rich history that birthed the labor movement, that made the middle class, and that has suffered too many collective tragedies. On December 5, 2020, nineteen students and I circumambulated Flint's biggest scar—the Buick City brownfield (417 acres of emptiness). By plotting a route and walking it, students learn to create new circuits that define and affirm Flint's value through the dialectic of moving back in time to remember and channel the heroism of past workers into new forms of industry, to recover personal family stories that expand the sense of relatedness into the community, and to share the experience of the poor and feel it to be full of spiritual opportunities. Encounters with the tragic sublime put us up against something like death, but we walk on beyond the flatline of the brownfield with what William Desmond calls "posthumous minds" uniquely sensitive to and appreciative of life. After the pilgrimage, students made story maps of their individual journeys that document Black and white Flint becoming a Flint of many colors—where the secret spirit of humanity lives on.

I taught this, my second iteration of the walking class that builds toward pilgrimage, during the pandemic (fall 2020). Ours was one of the few classes permitted to meet face-to-face because I planned to teach one day of the week in a park on campus or while we made exploratory walks to forgotten microregions of Flint. Though we had to wear masks while walking, a piece of cloth over the mouth and nose could not contain our delight at being able to share experiences and thoughts with one another after months of quarantine, and the pandemic context gave deep personal meaning to Antonia Malchik's point about the way walking builds social infrastructure: "When we venture outdoors, we put trust in ourselves as well as others. When we stay inside, we are mostly alone with ourselves and our thoughts. At home is where we have privacy; outside, we have to share with others."[4] Most of the students live with families in nearby suburbs, and a brief entry survey revealed that more than half of them had family members who had worked for GM and all had been taught to stay out of Flint by parents and relatives who stigmatized the city as bad, dirty, and dangerous. Factory workers moved their families out of Flint beginning in the 1950s, when housing was in high demand and the suburbs were expanding. Since then, Flint's decline as well as the call of better schools and safer (whiter) communities are the push and pull factors that led young families to buy homes and settle beyond the city limits. Coming back to Flint was, for many of these students, recovering their family roots. Two young women had great-grandfathers who participated in the 1937 Sit-Down Strike: one knew about it before taking the class, but the other found out only after talking to her family about what we were learning and where we were walking. The walks brought the past rushing back to another young man, who had grown up on

---

4. Antonia Malchik, *A Walking Life: Reclaiming Our Health and Our Freedom—One Step at a Time* (New York: Da Capo Press, 2019), 10.

the eastside in the 1990s and was raised by his grandmother, whose house died in a fire, probably set on purpose.

As a teacher of literature preparing to help students create and walk a pilgrimage route, I am perhaps hyperaware of the way that pilgrimage involves falling into and living a storied way walked by those who have come before us—a holy man or woman and their followers who mourn, celebrate, and worship. I prepare students for this experience by teaching them a practice that I call "walking books" that productively works against the polarization of reading and living and instead treats both as immersive experiences that are mutually enriching. The first part of the semester, we read philosophers, naturalists, theologians, and essayists who write about walking. Instead of working on texts in an academic way (analyzing and annotating), we reverted to the pioneer mentality advocated by Thoreau: be like the farmer with only a few words of Latin that stir the imagination while working in the field, and take one book to your cabin that frames and defines the way of life being lived there.

The habit of taking ideas from author guides and using them to create our own lines of thought and our own stories worked, too, when we turned our focus to Flint. For example, students found Thoreau's metaphor of the swamp a useful one for thinking about the wastelands and the tracts of ruined neighborhoods patchworked across the city. The swamp, for Thoreau, epitomizes wildness (men don't readily cross it); it is a place where trees fall and rot, and the natural process of decay makes a nutrient-rich bog out of which new life emerges. Flint's ruins—old silos and fragments of factories, cracked concrete shop floors, charred shells of houses with the detritus of life exposed in sidewalk shoals of mattresses, plastic trikes, and holiday decorations—exist as stains of blight with people living around them. These areas are no-man's-lands, and one student noted that when driving by them, they give the city a half-dead, zombified look that is horrifying. We run from zombies. But when we look through the lens of the swamp metaphor, we are reminded that decay is natural; damage is natural. Nothing that is perfect is truly alive, but all life exists in proximity to death. "In the slum, in some way, the direct voice of the heart is there," writes architect Christopher Alexander, who defines the elusive quality of "life" as "the force of direct human experience, misery, compassion, ignorance, and warmth all mixed up together."[5] Flint is rich and wild in the same way that any swamp in nature is rich, and Thoreau goes on to connect the actual swamp with our own inner wildness, "the bog in our brains and our bowels."[6] The other metaphor that my students found especially useful for reseeing Flint was Rebecca Solnit's idea that ruins become the unconscious of a city— "its memory, unknown, darkness, lost lands"—that truly brings it to life.[7] Disordered postindustrial cities that spring free of men's plans, maps, and manlocked sets welcome troubled people, forgive them their imperfections, and invite them to use the empty lots and blank, crumbling walls as a canvas for their creative imaginings. The Flint Public Art Project is doing this on a large scale: grants have enabled organizers to bring professional artists from Detroit, Britain, Europe, and even South America to paint over one hundred murals across the city that engage, stimulate, and help Flint people see the beauty, see human faces looking back at them instead of blank walls. But we need to teach ordinary people to do this on a small scale.

---

5. Christopher Alexander, "The Phenomenon of Life," in *The Nature of Order: An Essay on the Art of Building and the Nature of the Universe* (Berkeley: Center for Environmental Structure, 1980) 59–60.

6. Thoreau, "Walking," in *Walden, Civil Disobedience and Other Writings*, 3rd ed., ed. William Rossi (New York: W. W. Norton, 2008), 276.

7. Rebecca Solnit, *A Field Guide to Getting Lost* (New York: Penguin, 2005), 89.

In addition to the literary and theoretical lenses used for seeing Flint more imaginatively, it's also important to find a story from the past that students can connect with. In this particular class, it was the 1937 Sit-Down Strike, in which workers inside the auto plants literally stopped working for six weeks. During that time, they were victims of psychological manipulation, tear gas, and gunfire but were supported by the National Guard (called in by a governor who was determined that the strike should play out peacefully) and the Flint Women's Emergency Brigade, who supplied them with food, organized the wives to support the strikers against the police, and educated women on the need for a union. The outcome was a victory for the fledgling Labor Movement when GM recognized the United Auto Workers union, and it was a victory for all the ordinary people (some in students' own families) who stood up for the rights of workers to decent conditions and their families to basic social services. Most of the students in the class knew next to nothing about the strike and were later surprised that this enormously significant story had not been taught or even passed down by elders. We were also coming off a summer when young people had protested in cities around the country for recognition that "Black Lives Matter," but none of the students in my class raised their hands when I asked if they'd marched in the local protests. I introduced the historical event, and then I planned a group walk through the remediated brownfield to the Sit-Down Strike memorial on Chevrolet Avenue. By walking on the broken shop floor, overgrown with high grass that made Flint look like Kansas dipped in concrete, I wanted us to go beyond knowing the strike cerebrally to participating in it. To help that happen, I assigned a story by Meridel Le Sueur about the Minneapolis truck drivers' strike of 1934. The story describes the transformation of hyperindividualistic middle-class consciousness that must happen if one is to march or participate in any collective action. My hope was that my own students would see this group walk as a minipilgrimage, following in the footsteps of those early workers.

My intuition paid off, and in retrospect, I see that this trial run for the actual pilgrimage sensitized students to the spiritual energies in Flint and stimulated their desire to remake and rebuild. Most were saddened and many outraged by the erasure of history. They thought the few historical placards on Chevrolet Avenue that marked the Battle of the Running Bulls where police fired on strike supporters were "pathetic" or "not enough," and several expressed a longing for a ruined piece of the factory that would be a placeholder for the memory of these monumental events: "I never got to meet my great-grandpa or grandpa," lamented Melissa, "so I had hoped that going to these sites might make me feel connected to them in a way. It was gratifying to think that they had once been on that piece of land. But since it was much different than when they were on it, I did not really get the particular connection I was hoping for." The students learned in a sudden and visceral way that the past depends on the minds, imaginations, and industriousness of people here now. The emptiness made them wish the factory (or a piece of it) was still standing.[8] Ruins, plentiful in most urban landscapes, are a unique boon for the aspiring pilgrim. They are the skeletal structure of a place, and they "speak" all kinds of things—stories of change, of pain, of loss, and of human making and caretaking. Susan Stewart calls them the equivalent of the syntactical non sequitur: "They do not follow or precede—they call for the supplement of further reading, further syntax. . . . They call for an active, moving viewer . . . who

8. GM quickly tears down the plants it shuts down, erasing history in the process. There are traces of the enormous Chevrolet factory on the site: a cracked concrete floor, repurposed concrete benches, and concrete embankments along the Flint River that the US Army Corps of Engineers installed in the 1940s to protect the factories against spring floods.

can restore their missing coordinates and names."[9] The viewer's response, I believe, reveals much about their own essential spirit. My prompt for the "Walking Flint" essay invited students to "fill an empty space" or "paint a mural on a ruin," and I gave them options of writing a proposal for land reuse, reading a ruin by writing a story or series of poems, or making a picture and explicating it. Among the proposals for new strike memorials, workers' parks, and murals, there was one student's memory of seeing a red fox—his first fox ever—along the concrete embankment of the Flint River. Life—natural life—in postindustrial Flint is also a non sequitur that wakes us up to joy.

The traditional pilgrimage texts studied in the last unit of the course helped us improvise an urban pilgrimage insofar as they reminded us that when we self-consciously become pilgrims, our walking is rhetorical and our movements have meaning. Bunyan's *Pilgrim's Progress* as well as a Muslim student's stories about the hajj reminded us that the choices we make with our bodies matter—choices to go straight or take a detour, carry or lose our burdens, circumambulate, run between, kneel, prostrate ourselves, or leave an offering. But because we had yet to decide where in Flint we wanted to go, Vaclav Cilek's "Bees of the Invisible," with its "rules for wayfarers," proved most helpful because his work gave us permission to consider "sacred" small places that feel resonant and closed places—injured or damaged—that we must work to get to know.[10] When asked to journal about a place of spiritual signif- icance, one male student wrote about a "secret hideout"—a place "where WE [he and his friends] made the rules and WE decided

9. Susan Stewart, *The Ruins Lesson: Meaning and Material in Western Culture* (Chicago: University of Chicago Press, 2020), 2.
10. Vaclav Cilek, *To Breathe with Birds: A Book of Landscapes* (Philadelphia: University of Pennsylvania Press, 2006), 161–69.

what WE wanted to do when we were there." When he revisited his hideout as a college student, he admitted that it looked plain and abandoned, but it retained a sacred quality because of the experiences he had there: "Looking at the base nature of something is what spirituality is all about, I think."

A group walk around Thread Lake (abandoned now but once a recreational destination for workers) was the context for planning our pilgrimage. "We've talked a lot about Buick City, but we've never seen it," offered Brooke. Kellee liked the idea of doing part of the walk silently "so that we can all give our minds a rest and honor the twenty-seven thousand workers who worked there and were forced to move when the factory closed." Tim wanted us all to paint rocks with uplifting quotes and questions that we'd leave along the way. As the ideas came pouring out, I felt like we were in our own secret hideout, and with each suggestion, I felt student fingers working to lift the lid on Flint and on themselves. It was also marvelous that their ideas were in sync with my wish that we could partially circumambulate Flint's biggest scar, walk in solidarity with workers and displaced families, and synthesize the motives of mourning and protest. My hope was that students might feel that poverty has its own immaterial fullness and that real life is always lived amid ruins (not in plastic suburbs or gated communities).

Our pilgrimage took place on Saturday, December 5, 2020, with special approval of the university opening committee. Due to pandemic restrictions, we had to walk masked, stay outside, and carry our own food. It was a very cold, gray day, and we planned to walk nine to ten miles. Students knew the general route and that our two main goals were the Buick City brownfield and St. Mary's on Franklin Street where *Mary, Mother of Flint*—a Black Madonna— is ensconced in a roadside shrine. They had journaled about their personal goals for the pilgrimage, and they understood that

Mary, Mother of Flint, an icon painted for the water crisis.
A reproduction of the icon that lights up at night stands
in an outdoor shrine on Franklin Street at St. Mary's
Catholic Church. *Source:* Catholic Community of Flint.

afterward, they would have to tell the story of their own journey.
Before setting out, I reminded them, "Although we are all doing
this walk together, each individual's journey will be different." The
final project in the class would be to create a story map. It's important to introduce the assignment before the walk because it powers
the reflective work that is part of any pilgrimage, but the guide must
also downplay worry about the exact form the project will take.[11] I
reminded them, "Let's just see what happens," and "Focus on what
you see and feel." But I also suggested practices they could do along
the way to help them see more contemplatively: pause periodically
to take a picture, jot down a haiku, record a voice memo, find the

---

11. Yang and Maitland note that pilgrimage couples experience with a reflexive trend to
   narrativize the path taken. Yang and Maitland, "Urban Pilgrimage," vii.

right place to leave your painted stone, say a prayer, or just let things sink in.

"It felt like a journey," Luke said after it was over. "It didn't feel like the other walks. . . . It wasn't leisurely. It took time and effort." In retrospect, I think giving them only a general sense of the route was a good idea because it heightened the feeling of not being sure where they were going. They had to trust. For most of them, I think, the terrain felt very foreign and very much like a wilderness: "Flint is waay bigger than I imagined," "There's so much space," "I thought it would be more compact and feel more dangerous," but no, it's "the Sahara." They all reacted to the vastness of the brownfield. The eastside isn't much different: the once-busy main street has closed businesses, recently torched buildings, and many "missions." Against this backdrop of sublime bleakness, little things jump out and almost demand to be noticed or read. Despite the weather, the mood of the group was light and buoyant as we strung out along the way. There seemed to be an easy drift between sociability and thoughtfulness, and most of the conversations I overheard related to things noticed in passing: the gated community across from a ghetto, closed schools, so many churches, the juvenile detention center where one student learned "to do hair," sea gulls over the brownfield, "It really makes you think" whispered to a classmate, boxes of produce thrown out and rotting on the side of the road, the disappearing names on a neighborhood 9/11 memorial, the roadside food pantry, plastic flowers on a very old red house, one fresh coat of paint and a four-car garage in a cluster of houses with their roofs fallen in and porches collapsed, the Black Madonna, beds of sweet carrots under wraps, children's faces on a mural, their faces focused on soap bubbles and insects. Toward the end of the walk, we passed a building with a hand-painted sign over the door: "Flintopia." "What is in there?" students asked. And when we got to the elegant-looking pavilion in Kearsley Park, I heard one student marvel, "I can't believe this is even here." They began imagining what could happen here: prayer meetings and protests, concerts and shows. They made their way forward by noticing, contemplating, reading, following their feelings about the things they were seeing. Afterward, Max said the walk had changed his attitude toward the blight in Flint: "When you are walking by dilapidated houses, they are the only things you have to look at, and you realize that this is a city left alone, and people are doing the best they can. You learn to live with it and see it in a different way." In Flint, the ruins speak to tell the stories that GM, by quickly demolishing the factories, tried to silence. Melissa thought of her grandpa and great-grandpa on the walk by Buick City ("I got a lump in my throat"), and Derek, who'd spent his very young childhood on the eastside, felt it all come back once we passed the field where he remembered ("as if in a dream") playing soccer. Flint, for all of them, in one way or another, felt more like home after the pilgrimage walk.

Simply by being present on the streets in some of the bleaker parts of Flint, my students displayed curiosity, caring, and a kind of devotion. As we were wending our way along the brownfield, a driver from a passing car shouted out, "God Bless You!" and later one of the students commented, "I didn't know walking had that kind of power. It made me proud and made me want to keep going." When we arrived at St. Mary's—our first and only rest stop in a warm place—Father Firestone addressed the class and explained the genesis of the water crisis icon. But what resonated most deeply for many of them was Father Firestone's statement that "we [the church] are not going anywhere. Even though there are few congregants at Mass, it is important to have a presence." He told the students that he wanted an outside shrine that lit up at night because "right across the street is a crack house and a house of prostitution."

Father Firestone was emphatic: "We need to be here." In the icon, Mary is Black, and the children who bring water for her to bless are brown. "What ethnicity was Mary, anyway?" asked one curious student afterward. On the story maps of many, the church figures as the destination, the center point, the climax.[12] They felt peace. They felt safe. They responded to the beauty of the stained glass and the symbols that speak wordlessly of real mysteries. One of the students created a map that consisted solely of matching pictures with haikus. On the church page of her story, she placed two photos of stained glass: Jesus teaching and Jesus's crucified feet, nailed and bleeding:

The light shining through
As if to say, look this way,
Appreciate me.

Greater love than this?
I have seen none within man.
We must be better.

Jesus was ruined, crucified by the world, yet he and his church want to stay. The absurd beauty of this kind of commitment—this *love*—spoke wordlessly to many about the purpose of our walk and of the whole class.

The story maps reflected an effort to go beyond the surface, to map the invisible landscape of Flint's spirit, using pictures, poems, homemade symbols, and allegorical evocations. Several students explicitly connected their own pilgrim journey with Flint's story

---

12. I thought this was very interesting considering that we'd focused on nontraditional pilgrimage and perhaps indicates the way, in damaged urban places, churches really provide social salvation.

by using the landscape to describe their own internal worlds. One student's map was allegorical in a way reminiscent of Bunyan's *Pilgrim's Progress*. A small pilgrim figure moves through a series of very distinct places: there was "the valley brown and gray" where a "giant" (GM) had "consumed all it could find / Until, in desperation, having nothing else to consume / The giant consumed itself." This same student placed *Mary, Mother of Flint*, in the center of his map, standing tall among the rubble for the belief that "the hopeful heart that will someday clear the debris / Yet it remains to find what will do so for me." He later explained that he sought to make the church "allegorical for inner healing. . . . It's the idea that you can try to fix something from the outside but the real progress toward moving on in life for each person and for Flint comes from within." His concluding poem about finding a badly damaged penny—"it was a real thing from the walk"—speaks to the idea that Flint and the things in it have a real "rusty" beauty: "I thought the scars made it unique and different from all the other pennies":

> In the road along an intersection I happened upon a penny.
> It had been worn, scraped and warped
> And gashes through its face stripped it of its copper lining
> It wore the scars of some great trauma. Yet Lincoln's stoic
>   visage shone through the disrepair
> And while its shiny days are long past,
> It remains a penny all the same.

The student who most explicitly felt Flint's story in his own life noted that we must accept the good and bad variations as part of life and recognized that he didn't want "a Buick City situation" in his life but, he said, "That doesn't mean I should avoid change." By the time we got to the urban farm, the new cap he wore had messed up his hair, but he didn't care, since there was "no need to keep up appearances here. Just being together is enough." He, too, keyed in on Father Firestone's emphasis on the importance of presence when he wrote, "Many companies and people have bailed on Flint. . . . Its presence blights them. But Flint is more like its church than may at first seem. The presence of Flint is a reminder that we need to do better. We need to handle problems face-on, we must help one another, we must try to pick back up when we fall down. Without Flint, many people would easily forget issues of poverty, class and race divides, deindustrialization, abandonment of cities. Flint is a reminder, like the church reminds the lost, that there is work to be done."

Following the walk, one of the students asked me about volunteer opportunities, and he arrived four days later to help load boxes of food for the holiday into the cars of needy local people. I see, in retrospect, that walking to Buick City (the heart of a city's tragedy and pain) provided students with an encounter with the tragic sublime. Devastation of hundreds of acres. Ruination of thousands of lives. One student wrote that while walking, she thought about "the thousands of people that used to go in and out of there every day, each person with different lives they live and different experiences. How were these people affected when they lost their jobs? Did they lose their houses? Go into debt? Did they struggle to find new jobs or did they remain out of work?" Like their forefathers who daily had to fight to keep their sanity and humanity on "the line," my students saw firsthand the bleakness of abandonment in the face of corporate greed, and they saw that life, human and natural, struggles on, grows through the cracks. With "posthumous minds" that have come through death or near death, they experienced innocent delight in the feeling that "something will happen, despite everything, within this threatening void, that something will take place and will announce that everything is not over."[13]

In T. S. Eliot's poem "Journey of the Magi," which opens with the resonant line "A cold coming we had of it," the magi suffer and feel like they have undergone a death. They arrive at Bethlehem just in time to see the humble birth, but it isn't haloed with epiphanic light—the place was "you may say, satisfactory." The momentous change happens internally. They feel the birth as their own rebirth after death: "This birth was hard and bitter agony for us like death, our death." The incarnation—the birth of Christ (new life) with and in them—forever displaces these three wise fools, and my own hope is that my students, who had a change of heart about Flint and themselves, will walk on and take with them, wherever they go, the desire and the skills they need to sanctify places—especially damaged places, because as the poet John Milton has the archangel Michael say to Adam and Eve as they prepare to leave Eden,

God attributes to place
No sanctitie, if none be thither brought
By men who there frequent, or therein dwell.[14]

Questions for Reflection

1. What places in your city are resonant for you? How can the guide share them with the class?
2. What issues need to be addressed, or what needs to be healed in your city?

13. Jean-Francois Lyotard, *The Inhuman: Reflections on Time*, 84, quoted in Carol Newsom, *The Book of Job: A Contest of Moral Imaginations* (Oxford: Oxford University Press, 2003), 256.
14. Milton, *Paradise Lost*, book 11.

3. Are there stories or histories that would deepen pilgrims'/students' appreciation for the city?
4. Are there metaphors, concepts, or favorite texts from your discipline that might help students or pilgrims resee or see more feelingly their homeplace?
5. What borders—visible or invisible—or boundaries might be crossed and stitched together by a pilgrimage route?
6. If pilgrimage is the climax of lots of shorter walks, students may be very eager to do something or contribute in some way. Is there a cause for which the group would like to walk? My first time teaching the class, even though we had a destination, the students wanted to walk for "adolescent mental health," and so we wore badges that identified us as "Peace of Mind Pilgrims." Having a cause like this gives students a different kind of stake in the activity.

Select Annotated Bibliography

Cilek, Vaclav. "Bees of the Invisible." *To Breathe with Birds: A Book of Landscapes*. Philadelphia: University of Pennsylvania Press, 2006.

Czech geographer Vaclav Cilek lists his rules for pilgrims or wayfarers that help us think deeply about the connection between outer and inner landscapes and take seriously our interest in particular places that we may sacralize with our own homemade offerings.

Griswold, Wendy. *Regionalism and the Reading Class*, Chicago: University of Chicago Press, 2007.

Sociologist Wendy Griswold discusses the way place and region are created by people having experiences and writing about or mapping them with symbols. She suggests that places must be anchored or moored by stories about them, and her work is useful for thinking about the value of pilgrimage in urban contexts.

Lane, Belden C. *The Solace of Fierce Landscapes: Exploring Desert and Mountain Spiritualities.* Oxford: Oxford University Press, 2007.

The fierce landscapes that Lane (a Presbyterian minister teaching at a Catholic university) describes are readily transposed to damaged postindustrial places. He explores the relationship between inner and outer wilderness, in which the physical landscape is an integrant of selfhood.

MacFarlane, Robert. *The Old Ways: A Journey on Foot.* New York: Penguin, 2013.

MacFarlane turns every walk into a kind of pilgrimage because, as he notes, paths are acts of consensual making, and we are always on the trail of one who has come before us.

Maitland, Padma, and Lawrence Yang, eds. "Urban Pilgrimage." Special issue, *Room One Thousand*, no. 3 (2015). http://www .roomonethousand.com/3-urban-pilgrimage.

This issue explores what pilgrimage can mean in more secular contexts and how the routes and circuits of moving bodies seeking transformation can define and affirm new values. The introduction to the issue encourages us to consider new experiences and patterns of movement within urban environments that include dystopian voyages, protests, and the new urban sublime of postindustrial cities.

Pujol, Ernesto. *Walking Art Practice: Reflections on Socially Engaged Paths.* Charmouth, Dorset: Triarchy, 2018.

This is a collection of intimate reflections by a performance artist and former Buddhist monk. Short provocative pieces help us rethink what it means to walk as a cultural practice, a meditative practice, a radical practice. Parts 2 and 3, "Roadside Spiritualities," have several meditations on walking as an everyday pilgrimage when we attend to inner and outer landscapes.

Stewart, Susan. *The Ruins Lesson: Meaning and Material in Western Culture.* Chicago: Chicago University Press, 2020.

In this cultural history of the West's fascination with decayed remains, from Egyptian relics to contemporary monuments of destruction and trauma, Stewart explores why we are so drawn to the sight of what is broken, damaged, or decayed. Ruins excite our imagination with the lesson that our greatest structures will one day return to the ground while reminding us that in their fallen states, these sites are endowed with beauty, even redemption.

Conclusion

How to Use This Book

This book was written with a clear, practical purpose: to serve as a tool for pilgrim guides, teachers, and their groups. We had in mind groups that would be rooted in an academic institution (e.g., for a credited course or another formation initiative) or in a faith community (e.g., a congregation preparing itself for a pilgrimage to the Holy Land). Individual pilgrims who want to bring a reflexive dimension to their journey, either as preparation or post factum, would also benefit from this book. The contributors are at once scholars and pilgrims, bringing their experience to their scholarship and vice versa.

The book is divided into two parts. The first five essays emphasize various theoretical approaches to pilgrimages, whereas the following seven focus on different contexts. For each essay, questions are suggested that could be of use for the groups or the guides in addition to an annotated bibliography. The essays are meant to spark the imagination of teachers and guides. Some are more practical and could easily find an application in the context of a group. Others are more exotic and as such could offer an insightful counterpoint to one's experience or context. Some themes run across the essays: the motivation for pilgrimage, the role of the destination, the importance of the body, austerity and asceticism, the unfolding of time, the role of the arts, group dynamics between community and individual, the openness to encounter and transformation beyond expectation, and interreligious connections.

This book could be used in a variety of ways. Let us share some thoughts here:

> *Reflection and discussion.* All essays are relatively short and offer some questions to spark reflections. The questions are written to help deepen the content of the essays and to connect them with one's experience of pilgrimage. Each essay with all its questions could certainly be used independently in a single meeting. A guide could also change, combine, or prioritize some of the questions. The reflection could be planned either before (as preparation), during, or after the pilgrimage (as an opportunity to read one's experience).

> *Addition.* For each essay, an annotated bibliography offers some essential references to dive deeper into the perspective sketched. Some of these references were developed in the essays, but others provide new avenues. Teachers might want to leverage the bibliography to expand the intellectual scope and depth of their teaching. Similarly, guides and readers might find in them insightful suggestions for further exploration.

> *Order.* The order of the essays has its inner logic, especially through the two-part division in approaches and contexts. However, another order of exposition could be chosen. One could emphasize the contextual dimension, focus on the most far-flung experiences, or highlight a specific theme (e.g., interreligious) and group

the articles complementing the theme (e.g., around the use of art). A guide could use the essay that corresponds more closely to the experience of their group or, on the contrary, the most distant in order to stimulate reflection.

We hope that this dialogue between practice and theory and between different types of experiences will enrich the pilgrim journeys of many readers.

If you happen to use this book for a course or group preparation, do not hesitate to contact us to let us know the way in which you used it!

André Brouillette, SJ, and Jeffrey Bloechl